CANADIAN CRIME
INVESTIGATIONS
Hunting Down Serial Killers

Peter Boer

FOLK
LORE
PUBLISHING

© 2006 by Folklore Publishing
First printed in 2006 10 9 8 7 6 5 4 3 2 1
Printed in Canada

The Publisher: Folklore Publishing
Website: www.folklorepublishing.com

Library and Archives Canada Cataloguing in Publication

Boer, Peter, 1977–
    Canadian crime investigations : hunting down serial killers / Peter Boer.

Includes bibliographical references.
ISBN 10: 1-894864-60-3
ISBN 13: 978-1-894864-60-2

    1. Serial murderers—Canada. 2. Serial murder investigations—Canada.
I. Title.

HV6805.B64 2006   364.152'3092271   C2006-904909-2

Project Director: Faye Boer
Project Editor: Kathy van Denderen
Proofreader: Bridget Stirling
Cover Image: Courtesy of Bill Fritsch/Brand X Pictures

We acknowledge the support of the Alberta Foundation for the Arts for our publishing program.

We acknowledge the financial support of the Government of Canada through the Book Publishing Industry Development Program (BPIDP) for our publishing activities.

Canadian Heritage   Patrimoine canadien

PC:P5

Contents

Warning: Some portions of this book are of a graphic nature and may be objectionable to some readers.

Dedication

To all those who "maintain the right,"
thank you.

Acknowledgements

None of my success to date would be possible
without the help of my publisher, thank you for
your patience; to my father and brother, your
encouragement is always appreciated; to Shane,
for listening to my ideas and giving me the chance
to bring them to fruition; to my editor, Kathy van
Denderen, for her seamless editing and unwavering
attention to detail; to Warren Goulding, for sharing
his inside knowledge with me; and lastly, to the
men and women of Project KARE, for not just their
cooperation, but for their continuing efforts to bring
a killer(s) to justice—your commitment and
dedication are inspiring and humbling.

Introduction

THERE ARE NO ANSWERS IN THIS BOOK.

I am not a police officer, nor a psychologist. I am a journalist, author and history student. It is not my place, nor is it the place of this book, to try to answer one of society's most enduring questions—why do people kill.

Instead, the goal of this book to assemble into one work the stories of the Canadian men and one woman who were captured and those few who, to date, have terrorized the young and less fortunate and have violated one of humanity's most fundamental rules: thou shalt not kill.

Not all of the stories in this book are complete. Even as this work goes to print, one of the largest homicide investigations in the country's history is still ongoing. Since 1983, 21 Edmonton-area prostitutes have been killed, their bodies found mostly in rural areas to the south and east of the city. One man has since been arrested and charged with killing one of those women. Thomas George Svelka has been charged with second-degree murder and interfering with a dead body in the May 2006 death of Theresa Innes, whose remains were found stuffed in a hockey bag at a Fort Saskatchewan home.

Project KARE, a collaborative effort between the RCMP and Edmonton Police Service, is now responsible for investigating each death or disappearance of any woman who has led a high-risk lifestyle. Investigators have stated publicly that there is at least one offender, if not more, responsible for more than one of the killings and have released a detailed profile of the likely offender. To date, there have been no more arrests.

The work of Project KARE, however, highlights several fundamental social themes that run through many of the chapters in this book. Although not all of the murder victims in Edmonton have been prostitutes, most of them were. Not all of the victims were of First Nations descent, but several were. Not all of the women whose lives were cut short at someone else's hands were drug addicts, but many of them were.

Prostitutes are often the targets of serial offenders because of their frowned-upon status in society. Many of these women are not prostitutes by choice, but by necessity. They may come from broken homes or tragic backgrounds, forced onto the street either by circumstances beyond their control or by substance abuse issues they cannot overcome. They are so often the most forgotten members of our society, even though they may be in need of the most help. Too often when one of these women dies, the rest of us choose not to care. We see their demise as a product of the choices they made in life rather than as a function of the vicious triangle of drugs, mental and physical abuse and sexual aggression that dominate their everyday existence. The death of a prominent member of the community tends to make front-page news. However, it takes several similar killings of prostitutes and the haunting spectre of a serial killer among us before the rest of society starts to pay attention.

Such was the case in Vancouver, BC, up until 2002, when RCMP officers and forensic investigators descended on a Port Coquitlam farm belonging to a man named Robert William Pickton. In the 20 years previous, several dozen women had gone missing, most of them sex-trade workers. When their disappearances were reported, the subsequent police investigation often lacked the dedication typical of any other murder or missing persons report. Although the police finally formed the Joint Missing Women's Task Force and arrested Pickton, the effort came too late to save the lives of as many as 30 Downtown Eastside prostitutes. Pickton has since been charged with the murders of 26 of those women. He will stand trial before a jury on six of those charges in January 2007.

Prostitution is not, as is typically said, society's "oldest profession," but it has endured since biblical times, creating victims for men inclined to take advantage of the women involved in the trade. In 1890, Thomas Neill Cream, a Canadian-raised doctor, poisoned four prostitutes in London, England. Although he was convicted of murder and hanged, his legend endures because of his reported final words at the gallows, "I am Jack the..." Amateur historians fascinated with the Whitechapel, or Jack the Ripper, murders in 1888 have since postulated that Cream could have been the Ripper, despite strong evidence to the contrary.

Keith Hunter Jesperson, a Canadian by birth transplanted to the U.S. by his family, became known as the "Happy Face Killer" for his habit of signing the letters he sent to the authorities and newspapers during his killing spree with a happy face. Jesperson is currently serving four consecutive life sentences for murdering women in Oregon, Washington and Wyoming. He claims eight victims in total, many of whom were prostitutes who have not yet been identified because of their transient lifestyles.

John Martin Crawford's victims may or may not have been prostitutes, but they were all of Aboriginal descent, a fact that can often be ignored in Canada, especially in Saskatchewan. Aboriginal women are more likely to die a violent death than any other group of women in Canada, yet the police response to Crawford's crimes was slow and the media coverage of his trial lacking, for a man who killed at least four, if not more, women.

Apathy can also endure when it comes to the disappearance of our most vulnerable group in society, our children. In the early 1980s, Clifford Olson kidnapped, tortured, raped and killed almost a dozen children and teenagers, both boys and girls, in Vancouver's Lower Mainland. Yet because several of the children were known as runaways, the police did little to follow up their missing persons reports. Olson was eventually arrested and sentenced to life in jail, but his capture came months after some seasoned investigators suggested he might be worth taking a closer look at.

During their brief marriage, Paul Bernardo and Karla Homolka killed three teenage girls. Their case made international headlines because they were seen as such a perfect Anglo-Saxon couple, and their victims, one of whom was Karla's own sister, were young schoolgirls. The inhumane torture the pair inflicted on their victims, which they decided to capture on videotape, only whetted the public appetite for more coverage. Homolka's recent release from prison enraged the public because it reminded the entire country of how much she had gotten away with.

Allan Legere's victims, however, were not prostitutes or children. Legere was originally sentenced for killing an elderly woman in New Brunswick during a home invasion, then escaped from jail and killed four more people: three women and a priest. The ensuing manhunt terrorized the entire region of Miramichi until his eventual capture and trial.

All of these killers can likely be classified as psychopaths, yet not all psychopaths become serial killers. It is not the place of this book to debate why that is. Maybe arson, animal cruelty and bed-wetting are good indicators of future psychopathic behaviour; maybe abuse suffered as a child, unsatisfying sexual experiences or drug and alcohol use also play a factor. The general consensus, however, is that there is no all-encompassing answer for why people kill. There may be common threads, but each killer does so for his or her own reasons.

This book tells the stories of the investigations, of the police detachments and officers responsible for bringing each of these killers to justice. Some of those investigators made mistakes that could have saved lives, but one cannot control for every single factor when dealing with a person who does not believe in social norms. Ultimately, those who dedicate their lives to tracking down the Paul Bernardos and Allan Legeres of the world are worthy of as much respect and gratitude as society can muster. Their job is never easy and seldom glamorous. Sometimes they make mistakes. We can only hope that future investigations will learn from them.

I once heard someone opine the merits of the "discretionary bullet theory," the belief that everyone in life should be given one bullet in their lifetime that they can use as they see fit, without consequence. Although I do not totally agree with this theory, it does raise the question of what to do with the Olsons, Bernardos and Jespersons of the world after we catch them and prove their guilt. I would like to think our society has evolved past the need for capital punishment, but I know that I might think differently if it was my wife, my child or my friend who became a victim of some defective personality. The price of living in a liberal society is the possibility that someone can use their freedom to somehow affect yours. The value of any free country, however, can be evaluated by how many of those same freedoms are extended to society's worst offenders.

It is of little consolation to the families of the victims, but there is some sense of justice in knowing that all of those in this book who were convicted of their crimes (with the exception of the deceased Dr. Cream) will never again be allowed outside the walls of a prison.

In the meantime, our society can best protect itself by learning from the actions of past killers and reducing the number of potential victims available to future offenders. The best strategy to tackle the latter is through enhanced social programming. By getting children and prostitutes off the streets, by giving them the chance to live a proud, drug-free life, by discouraging johns from preying on their services, we can help prevent lives that are already hanging by a thin thread from snapping completely.

The reader might notice a lack of gore and sensationalism in this book, compared to other true crime books available on the market. It is not the intent of this work to re-victimize the families of those who have died, to inflict any more pain on the world or to give any of these killers anymore power over society. There are no answers in this book, only information.

In the end, information may be our best weapon against the men and women who kill for pleasure.

CHAPTER ONE

Clifford Olson
(1940–)

August 12, 1981

THE TENSION IN THE AIR WAS AS THICK AS THE UNDERBRUSH where the two RCMP officers were hiding. In the near silence of the wooded area just outside Tofino on Vancouver Island, the only detectable sounds were those of the RCMP's quarry and his newfound company.

The man, the one they were watching, was inside a vehicle—a rental car—passing a bottle to the two female hitchhikers he had picked up on the island earlier that evening. The girls sipped greedily, wiping their lips with the backs of their hands and giggling at the skinny, brown-haired man who had offered them a ride. They had no idea who he was, just that his name was Cliff. They also had no idea what he was capable of.

Suddenly, the officers felt their skin tingle in collective fright as the mood of their quarry suddenly changed. He grabbed the bottle from one of the girls, knocked back a big gulp and barked at one of them to get out of the car, telling her to "get lost."

The officers traded a glance and nodded at each other. They had to act. Subtlety and caution cast aside, they stood and crashed through the trees towards the trio, hands reaching back for their holstered sidearms.

"Hold it right there," one officer shouted at the man.

But it was too late. The career criminal was already moving, gunning the engine of the car. The two officers scattered as the passing car kicked up a dust devil of gravel and dirt, screaming back down the logging road towards the highway. Both officers gave chase on foot and drew their weapons, knowing the man they were after would not get far.

As they thundered down the road, coming at last to the highway turnoff, the officers quickly stopped and lowered their guns. The offending car was at a standstill, idling perpendicular to the police car that was parked across the turnoff, denying any other vehicle exit or entry. The man they had been watching was already lying face down on the ground while another uniformed member snapped a pair of handcuffs onto his wrists.

There was no sense of relief within the ranks of the police, however, as they escorted the man to the police car. They had their man, Clifford Olson, suspected killer of 11 Lower Mainland children, in custody.

But the question that haunted all of them was whether they could keep him there.

The peaceful silence of Christmas Day 1980 in Richmond, BC, was abruptly shattered by the wail of police sirens.

A man out walking his dog that afternoon had called police to inform them of a grisly discovery he had made during his jaunt. He had found a body at the back of a dump north of River Road.

Members of the RCMP and forensic investigators who arrived at the scene were met by the putrid stench of death and the deformed mass of a decaying body. Even before the body was removed from the scene for autopsy, investigators knew that the young female had died in a most horrific way. Her body was covered with deep stab wounds, 10 in total, and her throat had been slashed twice.

The body was quickly identified as that of Christine Weller, a 12-year-old girl from Surrey, BC, who had been reported missing by her parents one month earlier. Although the report was dated November 25, Christine was last seen on November 19, when she went to a mall near her home to hang out with friends. She had borrowed a bike from one of those friends to make it back in time for dinner at the Bonanza Motel, where her family was living. No one had seen her since, and because she had run away from home several times in the past, her family had not bothered to report her missing until almost a week later. Even then, Christine's reputation as a runaway infected the police investigation from the very beginning. They, too, had thought she was a runaway.

They were wrong.

The investigating officers of the Richmond police detachment had few leads to kick-start their investigation. They knew Weller was last seen with her friends at a shopping centre in Surrey around 5:00 PM and had left to have dinner with her family. At some point between the short bike ride from the mall to the Bonanza Motel, she had met her killer. Weller's murder was brutal and savage, but police had little information to turn them towards a suspect.

Four months passed with little forward movement in the investigation. In 1981, the balmy days of winter in the BC Lower Mainland grew longer as spring approached. Still, the changing seasons brought no new leads in Weller's murder, and her parents, overcome with grief, found no comfort in the warmer weather.

On April 21, 1981, members of the Surrey RCMP detachment again found themselves responding to a report of a missing teenage girl. Colleen Daignault, 13, had not been seen or heard from since April 15. Daignault had been living with her grandmother in Surrey. The spunky teenager's father lived in Saskatchewan, and her mother, the family thought, was currently living somewhere in Vancouver.

Daignault had been visiting a friend in North Delta the night she was last seen, and she was supposed to take a bus back to her grandmother's home that evening. When she didn't return, Daignault's grandmother called the police. Although officers took her statement and opened a file on the missing teenager, they believed she was a runaway, just as they had thought Christine Weller was in the days following her disappearance. Investigators believed that Daignault had either gone to Saskatchewan to be with her father or to Vancouver to try to locate her mother.

That same day, in a different part of the Lower Mainland, Daryn Johnsrude, 16, left his mother's Coquitlam house to buy cigarettes. The sandy-haired boy had arrived in BC only two days earlier, from Saskatoon where he lived with his father. His mother had flown him out to BC to visit her for a while, and Johnsrude fully intended to return to Saskatoon, finish the school year and move back to Vancouver to live with his mother.

Police never suspected that Johnsrude was a runaway; the fact he had arrived in Coquitlam only a couple of days before made it unlikely he had chosen to disappear. No one, however, had any idea what had happened to the teenage boy, until two weeks later, when his mangled, bludgeoned body was found in a dike near Deroche, east of Mission, BC. He had been beaten to death with a hammer.

Of the three children reported missing, two had met with foul play, but police were in no position to link the killings in any way. They had no witnesses, no leads and no suspects to pursue. Although all three victims were adolescents, only one was male. No one thought that Daignault had met with foul play. No one thought there was a serial killer at work in BC.

On May 19, 1981, Sandra Wolfsteiner, 16, left the home of her boyfriend's parents in Surrey with a lunch bag in one hand, holding up the thumb of her other hand to all the cars passing her along the Fraser Highway. The lunch was for her boyfriend, who

worked at an auto body shop in Langley, where Wolfsteiner lived with her older sister.

Wolfsteiner was last seen by a friend at the Langley
Royal Bank. Wolfsteiner had closed her savings
account, containing all of 96 cents, and told her friend
she had just gotten a new job.

On May 20, Wolfsteiner's father and boyfriend
reported her missing to police. When they found out
about her withdrawal from the bank, investigators
quickly assumed she too was a runaway. There was
no suspicion she had met with foul play. And the
authorities still didn't know they had a problem.

One month to the day after Wolfsteiner's friends
and family had reported her missing, police in Burnaby were dispatched to an apartment complex to take
a report of another missing child. Ada Court, 13, had
been at the complex the previous Saturday to babysit
her brother's two young children. Court had left the
apartment Sunday morning to catch a bus to meet
her 18-year-old boyfriend. The boyfriend called her
parents when she didn't arrive.

Despite the lack of evidence to the contrary, the
Burnaby RCMP refused to believe that Court was
a runaway. She was a responsible, reliable and cheerful
teenager who loved her family and enjoyed being an
aunt. None of her personal effects were missing from
her home or school locker. It was not like her, the
family told police, to just pick up and leave without
telling someone where she was going.

Although they didn't confess it to anyone, as the police left the apartment complex they had a feeling they were not going to find Court alive.

What they didn't know was that Ada Court's killer was living just down the hallway.

Clifford Robert Olson was born in Vancouver on New Year's Day, 1940, to Clifford and Leona Olson. The family moved to Edmonton, Alberta, and lived there for a short time before settling in a one-storey home in Richmond, BC, in the government-built community of Gilmore Crescent. Leona worked in a local cannery while Clifford Olson Sr. drove one of the last horse-drawn milk carts in all of Canada.

From the time he could walk and talk, it was obvious that Clifford Olson Jr. was going to be a problem for the people around him, especially his family. The brown-haired boy seemed to lack the moral compass of most young boys. "That Olson boy" was always ready to take advantage of people's trust, going door to door in Richmond trying to sell expired lottery tickets or stealing the money that residents had left on their porches for the milkman, such as Olson's own father. He misbehaved in class because he craved the attention; he bullied the other kids because it made him feel like a big man; and he terrorized the neighbourhood pets because he was bigger than they were. It was rumoured that he had even killed a neighbour's two pet rabbits.

Clifford's parents and the rest of the community were at first willing to shrug off his outlandish behaviour as that of an energetic rabble-rouser, but by the time he was 10, he was skipping classes, shoplifting from local stores and even breaking into other people's homes. At the age of 17, he was already doing serious time in BC's prison system: nine months for a break and enter.

Of the next 24 years, the holy terror of Richmond spent only 1500 days as a free man. He escaped custody roughly seven times during his adult criminal career but was promptly returned to jail each time, facing a bevy of charges for offences committed while at large. Up until 1979, each time Olson made parole or was released on mandatory supervision, it was abruptly terminated because he had committed some new crime. He stole and wrecked a powerboat. He robbed a Safeway and took the manager hostage. On one memorable occasion, he and an associate spent the better part of a night trying to crack a safe at a paper mill. When the boys decided to tip the safe over on its side to come at it from a better angle, the door flopped open of its own accord. The boys looked up and saw a sign posted on the wall that read, "THIS SAFE IS UNLOCKED AND CONTAINS NO MONEY."

But for all the months and years Olson spent under lock and key, he had never been more than a nuisance. His crimes, though serious, never caused injury. They were property crimes that violated the victims' sense of security but never violated them physically. Olson quickly turned into a product of Canada's criminal justice system; he'd walk in the front door of the prison then walk out the exit door months later. He received no counselling, and no one in the prison system made any real effort to rehabilitate the young man.

In 1974, while serving a four-year sentence for forgery and theft, Olson's criminal career took a violent, perverted twist when he raped a 17-year-old cellmate. It was the first step towards his development as a sexual predator. He fed his newfound perverted lust with the child pornography he was able to acquire in prison.

Whether locked up in prison, on the lamb or free from jail, Clifford Olson always looked out for himself, first and foremost. Even while he was serving his most recent prison sentence in 1976, he still tried to ingratiate himself with the authorities. He decided to become a snitch, informing on two inmates who had organized a plot to smuggle drugs into the Agassiz Mountain Prison. His popularity, already low among his fellow cons, plunged as other inmates began threatening him. Olson asked for and was given a transfer to the federal institution in Prince Albert, Saskatchewan, his reward for exposing the smuggling scheme.

Unfortunately for Olson, word of his reputation preceded him to the prisoners at the institution. The prison authorities, unaware of this fact, placed him in the general prison population upon his arrival. On February 13, 1976, nine days after his transfer, another inmate attacked Olson and stabbed him seven times.

Although Olson recovered from the attack, prison officials still felt his life would be in jeopardy if he remained in Prince Albert. They decided to move him, eventually housing him at the Oakalla Penitentiary in BC, two cells down from a man who would further turn Olson down the path of sexual perversion.

Gary Marcoux was a convicted sex offender, recently released on mandatory supervision, when he was arrested on Canada Day 1976 in the disappearance of nine-year-old Jeanna Doove. The next day, acting on information Marcoux had offered under questioning, police found Doove's body, tied to a tree. She had been sexually assaulted and killed.

Marcoux and Olson had served time together in previous years, so the two communicated frequently during their joint stint in Oakalla by passing notes back and forth. Olson originally agreed to provide Marcoux with an alibi in Doove's death by telling investigators the two had been smoking weed together. But Olson instead saw another opportunity to ingratiate himself with the police, approaching investigators with an idea in which he would solicit information on the murder from Marcoux in the notes they passed back and forth. His efforts bore fruit. Marcoux provided increasingly more detail in Doove's abduction, assault and murder, going so far at one point as to include a map of the area where Doove's body was found. Olson turned every single note over to the Crown attorneys prosecuting the case. He later testified at Marcoux's trial and was instrumental in helping the Crown secure a life sentence for Marcoux.

But the incident had a further, more sinister effect on Olson. The grisly description of Doove's assault and murder also fed Olson's growing perversion. Two years after helping secure Marcoux's conviction and being released earlier in July 1978 on mandatory supervision, Nova Scotia RCMP stopped Olson to question him about a complaint of an indecent assault on a seven-year-old girl. When he asked investigators if he could go back to his hotel to tell his friends where he was, Olson skipped town. He was later arrested in BC on an outstanding warrant, but the Crown prosecutors in Sydney, Nova Scotia, decided against bringing him back to Nova Scotia to face the charges there.

One month after his 1980 release from prison, Olson picked up a young boy travelling by bus in Richmond, took him to a hotel and raped him. He spent one month in jail that same summer when he decided to visit the BC Penitentiary, which was being closed down and demolished. An astute guard at the jail recognized Olson and, remembering there was an outstanding warrant for him for violating the terms of his release, placed him under arrest.

On June 7, 1980, Olson was again released. In the almost 20 sporadic years Olson had spent in prison, he had not received a single hour of counselling. Because he was never legally arrested in Nova Scotia, no one new he had graduated from habitual criminal to sexual predator.

The families of Vancouver's Lower Mainland were about to find this out.

Although the public didn't know it yet, Clifford Olson was already on the RCMP's radar by the first week of July 1981.

Two months earlier, on May 26, a local tow truck company alerted the Agassiz RCMP that there was a single-car accident just outside the city limits. A middle-aged man and a teenage girl were being taken from the scene of the rollover to Agassiz Modern Tire. When RCMP Constable Bill Hudyma responded to the wrecker, however, the man bolted, pulling the teenage girl with him.

Police then received a second phone call, this time from the Agassiz High School principal. A man and an obviously impaired teenage girl had burst into the school's office, hollering for a taxi. The pair then tried to enter the school's library, but they were refused entry.

Corporal Darryl Kettles responded to the second call, where the assistant principal pointed him in the direction the pair had run. After cruising around the area, Kettles spotted a man in a blood-spattered T-shirt at a taxi stand. Upon demand, the man handed over his driver's licence. His name was Clifford Olson.

Kettles put the girl, who could barely stand by herself, into his cruiser but then turned and, in disbelief, watched Olson make a run for it, without his ID. Kettles put out a bulletin for Olson then returned to the detachment where he lodged the girl, named Kathy Sallows, in cells. He thought she was just drunk.

Olson was arrested later that night, caught in a taxi heading back into Agassiz. When taken back to the detachment, Olson at first refused to talk, then admitted he had hired Sallows to work for him and had been on his way to Mountain Prison to visit a friend. Olson even offered the fact that he had been instrumental in having Gary Marcoux convicted.

Kettles later admitted in the book, *Where Shadows Linger*, that Olson gave him a "bad feeling" from the start. Kettles also found it strange that Olson's home address was only two blocks from where Daryn Johnsrude was last seen.

A call to the Vancouver RCMP Crime Index Section revealed that Olson had outstanding charges of rape, buggery, gross indecency and possession of a weapon originating out of Squamish. He also had charges of buggery and indecent assault on a 14-year-old Richmond boy. Kettles called Squamish and was told Olson had allegedly offered a local girl, Kim Werbecky, a job, then drugged and raped her. Werbecky escaped by locking herself in a gas station bathroom until Olson left.

Kettles also contacted the Mission detachment and offered his thoughts on Olson's possible ties to Johnsrude's disappearance. Two members and a technician made the trip to Agassiz to search Olson's car. The effort, however, yielded nothing.

Olson was released on a promise to appear, charged with impaired driving and contributing to the delinquency of a minor. Once Sallows recovered, police released her into the company of a family friend from nearby Sardis. The following day, Sallows' mother contacted Kettles, saying Olson had called her unlisted number. Olson wanted to know how Kathy was and if she needed a ride home, and that the job was still available if Kathy wanted it.

Later that day, investigators with Vancouver's Serious Crime Section interviewed Sallows in Sardis, at which time she handed them a small green pill, one of three that Olson had given her in the car. They had been drinking at the time, and Olson told her to take the pills "so you won't get drunk." She had pocketed one and taken two. Shortly afterwards, Sallows said she began to feel strange, as though she couldn't move her arms or legs. A report issued a month later identified the pills as chloral hydrate, a sedative referred to on the street as "knock-out drops" or a Mickey Finn.

Three weeks after Olson was charged and released, Ada Court disappeared, and police were searching frantically for her. On July 2, 1981, police added another name to their growing list of missing Lower Mainland children when nine-year-old Simon Partington was reported missing in Surrey. He had left his house on his bike to go to a friend's house but never arrived. The police and public scoured the area but came up with only one clue: the owner of a fish and chips restaurant told investigators that she had seen Partington eating with a "gorgeous" blond man the day the boy disappeared.

Investigators scampered off in all directions, searching for the man, but they never found him. Two weeks after Partington's disappearance, his father, Stephen, received a phone call, demanding he pay a ransom for his son's safe return. With officers watching him every step of the way, Stephen followed instructions and made the money drop at a BC Hydro box. Police swooped in when two youths moved in to collect the cash. The boys, however, had nothing to do with Partington's disappearance and were later charged with extortion.

Olson, in the meantime, grew increasingly bold. He was arrested on July 3 in Burnaby for allegedly raping a teenage girl named Sandra Docker. Olson had approached the girl and her friend, Rose Smythe, the day before, offering them work. When the two girls met him at the Lougheed Mall the next day, Olson explained that he only had enough work for one of them, and he chose Docker. When he and Docker left, they drove to a liquor store for some whisky, drove to Surrey so Olson could exchange his vehicle at a rental agency for a different one, then pulled off in a secluded area to drink. It was then that Olson tried to rape Docker. She resisted. A livid Olson drove her back to the mall and dropped her off, where she promptly flagged down the first police car she saw. Soon afterwards, a Burnaby RCMP cruiser pulled Olson over and arrested him on charges of sexual assault and impaired driving. Olson was again lodged in cells and interviewed, where he again explained his role in Gary Marcoux's conviction. Corporal Les Forsythe, a member of the Burnaby detachment, noted that Olson lived within spitting distance of Ada Court's brother.

Despite their suspicions, Surrey investigators, who had jurisdiction over the case because it had occurred in their municipality, declined to move forward on the sexual assault charge, citing Docker as a "poor witness." Olson was once more released on a promise to appear.

Forsythe, however, was still troubled by Olson, both by his demeanour and his proximity to Ada Court the night she disappeared. He also noted how close Olson lived to where Daryn Johnsrude was last seen alive. On July 8, Forsythe did a helicopter search of the area around Surrey for fresh graves but came back empty-handed. He stopped in at the Mission detachment to share his thoughts on the Johnsrude disappearance with investigators. The members told Forsythe that Olson was a suspect, and they also shared with him the circumstances of Olson's May arrest in Agassiz involving Kathy Sallows. The group decided another meeting with representatives of the surrounding detachments might be a good idea and tentatively scheduled it for July 14. It was later changed to July 15.

Two days before the meeting, police in New Westminster received a phone call from a local apartment manager. The woman had received a bizarre telephone call in which she could hear only the sound of a young girl whimpering, moaning and crying. The sounds never stopped, even when the manager tried to talk to the girl. She later said it sounded like a tape recording.

The woman also said it sounded like the voice of Judy Kozma, 14, who had just recently moved into the building with her parents. When police investigated the call, they learned that Kozma had not been seen since July 9, when she had left home to meet a friend. The two girls were planning on taking a bus into Richmond to apply for a job at a Wendy's restaurant. Kozma, however, never made the trip.

Members of the surrounding detachments, unfortunately, were not aware of this latest disappearance when they convened in Burnaby for their July 15 meeting. Members from Vancouver Police, New Westminster Police and the RCMP detachments from Burnaby, Surrey, Coquitlam, Richmond, Squamish and Vancouver RCMP's Serious Crime Section all attended. One BCTV reporter, having caught wind of the meeting, even solicited a statement from Les Forsythe, who described the meeting as a "brainstorming session" on missing persons investigations.

A "procedural error" kept the New Westminster police representatives from sharing the news of Kozma's disappearance. The remaining investigators all batted around their own cases, wondering if Olson could be a suspect in the disappearances of Christine Weller, Ada Court and Daryn Johnsrude. Richmond police said they had a good suspect in Weller's disappearance but agreed the case fit the profile. Serious

Crimes told the assembled investigators they had two suspects in Johnsrude's case, but that they were also looking at Olson.

Forsythe described Olson's court disappearance, then the Docker assault. Squamish then briefed the group on Kim Werbecky's abduction and rape, while Coquitlam described the Kathy Sallow incident, as well as another disturbing development. Olson, they told the group, had married Joan Berryman on May 15, 1981. The night before, Olson had agreed to watch a group of kids while Berryman and her friends went out. Olson sent the majority of the kids to a nearby store for bubblegum, save for one five-year-old girl. The girl's mother later informed police that her daughter had told her Olson had assaulted her.

When the meeting broke up, all in attendance agreed that Olson should be treated as a suspect. A profile on him would be compiled, and Burnaby RCMP would keep an eye on him.

Olson, however, was nowhere to be found. He had taken his wife and child on a summer vacation to Knott's Berry Farm in California.

What followed turned out to be one of the most contentious points of debate about the investigation into Olson's activities. After verifying that Olson was out of the country, Forsythe filed a formal request for use of the RCMP's Special "O" Section, a unit that specializes exclusively in watching or tailing persons of interest. Forsythe filed the request with Burnaby GIS Staff Sergeant Bill Howitt, who contacted Special O and asked for assistance. The commander of

Special O initially authorized the use of one car per shift, but Howitt allegedly called back and cancelled the request. According to the book, *Where Shadows Linger*, Howitt was required to allocate one of his officers per surveillance shift to ride along with the tail car, something he didn't feel he had the personnel to do. Instead, Howitt contacted the Joint Forces Operation (JFO) group, an investigative branch of the RCMP, and asked for their assistance.

As the Mounties argued over surveillance, Olson returned to town, fresh from his vacation. Already another child was reported missing: Raymond King Jr., a 15-year-old boy from New Westminster, who was last seen riding his bike to the local Manpower office to find work. Police immediately knew something was wrong because they found King's bike abandoned at the Manpower office.

Within hours of King's disappearance, Constable Dennis Tarr stood inside the Olsons' apartment, chatting with the suspect. He did not confront Olson directly, however. Olson had offered previously to work as an informant for the police, providing he was paid well. Tarr showed up to discuss the idea with him but instead listened as Olson pulled out a newspaper article detailing Simon Partington's disappearance. Olson wanted to know how credible an alleged eyewitness to the crime was, then offered his own theories about what might have happened to the boy. One of those theories included a serial killer.

The two parted ways, agreeing to meet on July 29 to discuss the matter further. On July 24, Sigrun Arnd, a German student touring BC, disappeared in Coquitlam. Her disappearance went undiscovered for weeks because she was a foreign student travelling alone.

Three days later, on July 27, Terri Lynn Carson, 15, from Surrey disappeared. She had left her home early that morning to catch a bus to the north side of the city to apply for a job at a pet store. Carson's mother contacted police that evening and was told she had to wait 24 hours before filing a missing persons report.

The police, however, were already on Olson's tail. A surveillance team organized through JFO had spent most of the day trying to locate him. They finally found him just after 4:00 PM, hours after Carson had disappeared. The officers tailing Olson were under orders to arrest him the instant any young person entered his vehicle.

Two days later, on July 29, Constable Tarr met with Olson again, this time in the company of Randy Ludlow, a young man whom Olson had befriended. During their conversation, Olson hinted he might be able to provide information on the growing number of Lower Mainland missing children cases. The information, Olson said, could make Tarr's career. He just wanted to be sure he was well paid for it.

Tarr and Olson agreed to meet again in a few days. Hours after leaving his meeting with Tarr, the JFO surveillance team watched as Olson picked up a pair of young female hitchhikers. Acting on their orders, the team moved in and arrested Olson, who they found plying the two teenage girls with beer. He was charged with contributing to the delinquency of a minor, lodged in cells and released the following day so he could keep his meeting with Tarr.

Members of the JFO team were furious that Olson had been released. The move had also compromised their surveillance as Olson now most likely knew he was being followed. The team abruptly called off its surveillance.

Both Tarr and two other officers who accompanied him the next day wore wires as they sat across from Olson in a restaurant, recording everything he said. Although the officers baited him with possible rewards of up to $100,000, Olson refused to disclose any information on any of the missing children cases. He maintained he had been talking about drugs in his earlier meeting with Tarr, not bodies. Olson left the meeting promising he would "ask around."

Later that same night, a woman called the RCMP detachment in Maple Ridge, reporting that her sister, Louise Chartrand, 17, hadn't arrived at work for her night shift at a restaurant.

The RCMP now knew they had a serious problem on their hands. Five days earlier, police had recovered a corpse at Weaver Lake, near Agassiz. The body was so bloated and decomposed that it could only be identified through dental records. Those records confirmed the body was that of Judy Kozma. The autopsy revealed she had been stabbed repeatedly.

The RCMP moved into high gear, appointing Superintendent Bruce Northorp head of a special task force investigating the Lower Mainland missing children cases. The force met on July 31 and compiled a list of possible missing children, as well as a short list of three suspects, with Olson heading the list. The task force also received approval for Special O surveillance on Olson once he returned from a trip to Alberta.

That same day, police recovered a bra on the side of a road near Whistler belonging to Louise Chartrand. Three days later, they found her shirt and dress pants about 10 kilometres north of the resort town. On August 5, a police dog led a search party to another body, located only 1.5 kilometres from where Judy Kozma's remains were found. The following day, the corpse was identified as Raymond King Jr., who disappeared from New Westminster on July 23. The cause of death was ruled as "multiple skull fractures." The autopsy also noted that a 3.5-inch nail that had been pounded into King's head was not the cause of death.

The task force issued a plea to the public for information on any of the missing children cases and were rewarded with both a flood of tips and a mountain of scorn. While officers waited for Olson to return to BC from Alberta so they could re-establish contact, the public began venting its fear and frustration to the media. Chris Burgess, a friend of the King family, criticized the investigation's speed and thoroughness, going so far as to hire a private investigator of his own, then publicly asking Prime Minister Pierre Trudeau to call out the army.

An army of police officers, however, was waiting for Olson when he returned to BC on August 6. The following day, they tailed him as he drove to Coquitlam and rented a new car. The police towed away the vehicle that Olson had dropped off at the rental agency for processing for evidence. Over the next five days, officers scooped a 13-year-old girl Olson had driven past repeatedly, then watched as he followed an undercover female officer. He broke into a home in Burnaby, and on August 11 broke into two Vancouver homes, making off with small handfuls of cash. And still the surveillance unit watched. The next day, Olson took a ferry to Vancouver Island, invaded two more homes in Victoria, and made his way north. When he approached Nanaimo, Olson pulled over and picked up two female hitchhikers.

The nervous tension in the tail cars ratcheted up several notches as Olson drove north to Tofino and pulled off the road so he and his two new friends could drink. Several members were watching from the trees when Olson's mood suddenly changed. He ordered one of the girls out of the car, telling her to "get lost." At that point, the decision was made to move in. Olson saw the officers coming and stepped down on the gas, trying to get away. The road, however, was blocked by several police cars. Olson was handcuffed, placed in a police car and driven away to Ucluelet, where he was charged with impaired driving.

Although the police had a strong feeling Olson was responsible for several, if not all of the missing children cases, they had little evidence to prove it. Much of what they had was conjecture, circumstance and seasoned police inferences that, as of yet, were not backed up by any physical evidence or eyewitness testimony. The team was prepared to release Olson the following morning when a search of his car yielded their first solid piece of evidence: a notebook found inside contained Judy Kozma's name.

The following day, police flew Olson to Burnaby and charged him with two burglaries he had committed while being tailed. With Olson safely in custody, investigators now faced the daunting task of convincing him to testify. Kozma's name in his address book was a bullet in their magazine, but only one of few they could use against him. To truly make the case, the police had to get him to confess.

Olson wasn't making it easy for them. Over four days, several different officers took turns at him, hammering him with question after question. Olson did not request a lawyer, and instead sat in the interview room, smoking White Owl cigars and offering various explanations for his whereabouts or behaviours on any particular day. The police recorded and quickly investigated each alibi, the results of which were forwarded to Olson's interrogators so they could break down his stories. Olson held up but over time slowly began to weaken.

On August 18, 1981, he appeared in court in Burnaby again, where the Crown announced three new sexual assault charges. Olson was returned to custody for another round of questioning, but this time the police had more to work with. Investigators had tracked down Randy Ludlow, the sandy-haired youngster who had accompanied Olson to his July 27 meeting with Tarr. Ludlow confirmed that he was with Olson on July 9, the day Judy Kozma went missing. Ludlow explained that Olson had picked Kozma up, then dropped Ludlow off and driven away. The youngster also told police that Olson had drugged and raped him in late July.

It was the one solid piece of information that turned the investigation on its head. When investigators confronted Olson with the statement, he asked to see a poster drawn up by the task force that listed all of the missing children in the Lower Mainland. As he examined the poster, he began pointing at individual photos, muttering "this one...this one..." and glossing over others. He demanded to speak with someone with a position of authority, and Northorp, commander of the task force, was brought in to talk to him. Olson told Northorp he might be able to give the police some information if it could be guaranteed he could serve out his sentence in a psychiatric hospital. Northorp rejected the idea on the spot. With Kozma's name in the notebook and Ludlow's statement, Northorp ordered a charge of first-degree murder be laid against Olson.

Whether he was spooked by the charge or knew there was no way out for him, Olson began to cooperate. He implied that he was responsible for the murders of Raymond King Jr., Daryn Johnsrude, Judy Kozma and Christine Weller. He also implied he was responsible for the deaths of Terry Lynn Carson, Simon Partington, Ada Court, Louise Chartrand, Sandra Wolfsteiner and "a girl from West Germany," but he often spoke in the third person, shrewdly dancing around his own involvement. He offered a full confession in exchange for a deal that would let him serve his sentence in a psychiatric hospital. The police, however, could not guarantee any such arrangement because sentencing was the jurisdiction of the courts.

On August 20, Olson finally cracked. In what proved to be the most controversial aspect of the case, he suddenly blurted to investigators, "I'll give you 11 bodies for $100,000. The first will one be a freebie."

The very idea of paying a criminal to confess to his crimes ran against every fibre in Northorp's body, as well as those of his task force. Several officers, however, argued in favour of it. It was no different, some felt, than paying a snitch for information and would allow the police to close almost a dozen missing children cases. It would bring closure to the families of the victims and return a sense of security to Vancouver's Lower Mainland.

In the end, the assistant deputy attorney general for BC approved the deal, with the caveats that the money would be placed in trust for Olson's wife, Joan, and that the Crown would try to recover the money from her after Olson's conviction was assured.

The deal drafted by the Crown and signed by Olson on August 26 agreed to pay him $10,000 each for the bodies of seven victims, as well as an additional $30,000 for the personal effects of three more, for a total of $100,000. That same morning, operating on a schedule drafted by Olson, a team of heavily armed officers and dog men set out to begin the grisly search. Olson was handcuffed to another officer, and all of his conversations were recorded.

By 3:00 PM, police found Louise Chartrand's remains near Whistler. The next day, Simon Partington's body was found near Richmond. A third body, that of a female, was found weighted down in a ditch near Partington's. Hours after Northorp confirmed for the media that two bodies had been found, Olson led investigators to Terry Lynn Carson's remains, as well as some of Judy Kozma's personal effects. At 7:00 PM that night, Northorp was informed that officers had found some more human remains, most likely belonging to Ada Court.

It was as grisly a day as could be remembered in the halls of the RCMP, yet the bad news kept coming. The following day, Olson led his handlers to the body of Sigrun Arnd, the German tourist. Her body was found in a trench a mere 450 metres away from where Partington's body was found the day before. With each body or personal effect that turned up, another $10,000 was placed into Joan Olson's trust account. By August 28, she had collected $80,000.

Only the bodies of Colleen Daignault and Sandra Wolfsteiner had yet to be recovered.

Olson hinted that he could lead police to two other bodies, belonging to victims unrelated to the Lower Mainland murders. Both cases, however, had already been closed, and police concluded Olson was only trying to get his outstanding $20,000. That $20,000 dwindled to $10,000 when overanxious investigators believed Olson could lead them to the bodies of two more 16-year-old girls. The claim was never substantiated.

On August 31, police laid eight charges of first-degree murder against Olson. As the task force continued to investigate, they laid two more charges.

Over two weeks later, they turned up a hammer believed to have been used to kill Daignault. Her body was finally located near Surrey the next day.

The medical examiner's report detailing all nine murders read like a macabre shopping list, fleshed out by details Olson provided to investigators. Daryn Johnsrude was beaten to death with a hammer. So too were Raymond King Jr., Louise Chartrand and Sigrun Arnd. Olson had tried to kill Colleen Daignault by injecting air bubbles into her bloodstream, then had simply beaten her to death, again with a hammer. He strangled Simon Partington, Ada Court and Terry Lynn Carson. He stabbed Christine Weller and Judy Kozma to death.

Olson entered a plea of not guilty in federal court and was ordered to stand trial on 10 counts of first-degree murder on January 13, 1982. A courtroom packed with media and the families of the victims waited in hushed anticipation as the trial entered its first phase, known as a voire dire, basically a trial within a trial allowing the judge to rule on the admissibility of evidence. The first witness, Constable Dennis Tarr, offered some testimony, then played for the court the tapes he had made of his meetings with Olson when he was trying to cultivate the accused as a source. As the tapes played on, Olson became increasingly agitated and shifty. After two hours of testimony and a lunch break, Olson disrupted the court proceedings when he tried to approach Crown prosecutor John Hall. Justice Harry McKay ordered the lawyers for both sides into his chambers, then emerged and unexpectedly adjourned the proceedings until the following day. Outside the courtroom, Hall told reporters the trial would likely be "somewhat foreshortened."

The next day, Clifford Robert Olson stood in court and changed his pleas from not guilty to guilty. He also offered a guilty plea to an 11th charge of first-degree murder in the disappearance of Sandra Wolfsteiner.

The jury now had only to decide whether or not to accept the plea. The 12-person body, who had faced months of isolation for the duration of the trial after McKay had ordered them sequestered, quickly returned with their decision to accept the plea.

McKay promptly sentenced Olson, the confessed serial killer of 11 children, to 11 life terms in prison, without eligibility for parole for 25 years. It was the harshest penalty available to him under the Criminal Code of Canada.

"I would not normally presume to express my views to the National Parole Board, but in this case my considered opinion is that you should never be granted parole for the remainder of your days. It would be foolhardy to have you at large."

And with that, Clifford Olson left the courtroom to begin serving out his sentence.

The case, however, would not fade from the public eye. No sooner had Olson reversed his pleas than the story of the "cash for corpses" deal became public. Pundits and observers came down on both sides of the issue, supporting and criticizing the move in equal numbers. The media aired the missteps of the RCMP in the public eye, questioning the force's decision not to solicit the services of the Special O Section earlier, and the length of time it took to develop Olson as a suspect.

As soon as the trial ended, the government abandoned its attempts to recover the money paid to Joan Olson. A group of families of the victims started a court action to recover the funds and were initially successful when a judge ruled in their favour. That ruling was later overturned on appeal in 1986 and effectively killed when the Supreme Court of Canada declined to hear the case. The decision was another slap in the face to the families who had already endured so much. Two of the victims' mothers had their welfare cheques reduced by the province because they could no longer claim their dead children as dependents.

Olson soon became the scourge of the RCMP, the courts and the prison system. He launched an appeal of his verdict three weeks after he pleaded guilty then abandoned it altogether. He continued to hint that he had participated in other murders, such as the 1981 killing of Ogang Ngoc Ha at Golden, BC, despite the fact he was in custody at the time. He said he had killed Suzanne Seto, a realtor from Vancouver, even though Kelly Toop was convicted of her murder in 1982. Whenever Olson talked, however, the RCMP was obliged to listen. In November 1982, they flew Olson to BC from Kingston to search for more bodies. None was ever found, and Attorney General Allan Williams promptly declared to the media that Olson was "not credible."

Olson wrote letters to the media, claiming responsibility for some new murders and then denying other murders to which he had already confessed. In 1996, Saskatchewan RCMP flew Olson out to their province to discuss three murders in the province to which he laid claim. As usual, Olson produced nothing of substance.

In 1997, he filed a motion under Section 745 of the Criminal Code, applying to have his parole eligibility reduced. At the hearing, Olson claimed responsibility for 143 total killings, 64 of which occurred in Canada. He told the review body he and a friend were responsible for the Green River murders, even though most had occurred after he had been sent to jail. Gary Leon Ridgeway was charged in 2001 with the Green River murders.

Dr. Stanley Semrau, a psychiatrist who examined Olson, testified at the review, stating Olson claimed to have sexually assaulted hundreds of children and that he spent his time in jail writing a seduction manual. He was incapable of remorse, Semrau said, and was totally untreatable. Semrau described Olson as "the most disturbing personality I have ever encountered."

The judicial review jury agreed, and in 15 minutes they denied Olson's application to shorten his parole eligibility. The jury also went one step further, declaring Olson not be allowed to apply for parole again until he had served the full 25 years.

That day came on July 18, 2006. Family members of Olson's victims and several members of the media packed the hearing room at Sainte-Anne-des-Plaines, Québec, for his parole hearing. Some family members of the victims read out victim impact statements, while others who did not attend submitted them by mail. The hearing got off to a strange start when Olson requested he be transferred to a prison in the U.S. because he had secret knowledge of the 9/11 terrorist attacks on the U.S., but the board cut him off before he could continue giving his statement.

"No one can murder my memories," victim Daryn Johnsrude's sister said in her statement. "But it's not right that that is all I have, memories."

After being taken out of the room so that the parole board could debate its decision, Olson refused to return. In his absence, the board unconditionally denied his request for parole.

"You sadistically killed the victims, eight female children between 12 and 18 years old and three male children between 10 and 16 years old, over a period of eight months from November 1980 to July 1981," the board wrote in its decision. "You seem to be comfortable with your criminality and continue to demonstrate no remorse or empathy for the victims and their families.

"You continue to present a very high risk of recidivism. In light of these findings, the Board denies you any form of release as it considers that you continue to pose a clear and present danger to society."

As of the writing of this book, Clifford Olson is incarcerated at Corrections Canada's Special Handling Unit for violent and dangerous offenders, located at Sainte-Anne-des-Plaines, Québec. He will next qualify for a parole hearing in July 2008.

CHAPTER TWO

Allan Legere
(1948–)

November 16, 1989

THE GATHERED WORSHIPERS AT THE CHURCH OF THE BLESSED Virgin Mary in Chatham Head, New Brunswick, were starting to wonder where their priest was.

It wasn't like Father James Smith to be late, yet it was already several minutes past 7:00 PM, and no one had yet seen him. Even the first parishioners who had arrived early had found the church empty, the lights off. Some sat in the dark, waiting for Father Smith to appear, but he never did.

At 7:10 PM, a parishioner who often helped Father Smith around the parish with odd jobs, decided to go looking for him. Using his key, he let himself into the church's rectory. The second he walked in the door, he knew something was terribly wrong.

The floors and the walls of the rectory were covered in blood. The kitchen table lay on the floor, smashed to pieces. There was no sign of Father Smith.

"Someone call the police!" he shouted.

The response was instantaneous. Two RCMP cruisers pulled up to the church within minutes. While one officer taped off the area with yellow crime-scene tape, Sergeant Jacques Ouellette searched the rectory, gun drawn, flashlight piercing the evening gloom.

He poked his head into the study and stopped. Father Smith's broken, bloodied body lay on the floor. Ouellette touched a finger to the body, searching for a pulse. There was none.

Inside the church, Smith's flock was praying as hard as they dared that Smith was all right, even though they knew deep in their hearts he wasn't. As word began to circulate through the crowd that Father Smith was dead, a name began to join the whispers as it worked its way from the church to the town, to neighbouring Newcastle and all of New Brunswick. The RCMP flooded the streets with officers and police dogs, looking for the attacker's trail. They set up roadblocks on provincial highways, searching every car for one man. Their efforts, however, yielded no results.

Allan Legere, the "Monster of Miramichi," had struck again.

❧❦❧

The guards escorting Allan Legere to Dr. Georges L. Dumont Hospital on May 3, 1989, did not know their ward was an escape risk.

They knew who Legere was. It was impossible to live in New Brunswick and not know about him. His second-degree murder trial two years earlier had been front-page news in the Miramichi area, at the time a grouping of villages and towns dotting the Miramichi River in New Brunswick, with a population of 50,000. Legere was serving a life sentence with no possibility of parole for 19 years for the June 1986 murder of John Glendenning.

Everyone knew the story because both of Legere's accomplices in the home invasion had pleaded guilty before the trial began. On the night of June 21, 1986, John and Mary Glendenning walked the few metres to their home from their general store in Black River Bridge, 30 kilometres east of Chatham Head. Some time around 10:00 PM, three men burst through the Glendennings' door, attacking the couple viciously and demanding to know the combination to the couple's home safe. One of the men waited downstairs with John while the other two hauled Mary upstairs to the safe. Although she'd tried to open it, one of the men kept hitting her again and again until she eventually passed out.

When she pulled her head out of the toilet shortly after midnight, all she could manage to do was call the police. She was badly beaten, bleeding from her nose and mouth, and there was a scarf tied around her neck that wasn't there before. Her underwear was missing.

Mary's daughter and son-in-law, who were summoned by the police dispatcher, arrived before the first officer. The normally quaint family home resembled the set of a horror movie, with blood speckling the walls, dripping from the ceiling and congealing on the floor. The Glendennings' safe, containing approximately $45,000 in savings, was missing.

The missing money wasn't the tragedy. The first police officer who responded to the scene found John Glendenning's body on the floor of the master bedroom. He was covered in blood, his hands tied behind his back with the chord from a nearby digital clock. There was a shirt around his neck, tied so tight it was later revealed to have broken his Adam's apple. His nose, cheek and right jaw were also broken, as were several toes and fingers. The imprint of a boot was clearly visible on his head.

Mary was quickly taken to Hôtel Dieu Hospital, where doctors examined the battered woman. Her forehead was cracked, her nose was broken and one eye was swollen shut. She was covered in bruises, had a damaged lung and an internal injury to her arm.

As grisly as these injuries were, they did not compare to the conclusion doctors came to after examining her. Mary Glendenning, 61, had been raped with the barrel of a gun.

The police investigation got a kick-start hours later when a woman called the RCMP and informed investigators that three men, Todd Matchett, Scott Curtis and Allan Legere had left the area with close to $35,000. It was rumoured they had gotten the money after knocking over a safe. Minutes later, the same woman called back, describing the three men's destination and the car they were driving.

Matchett, 18, and Curtis, 20, were known to police, having both recently faced charges of theft, breaking and entering and vandalism. At the time of the Glendenning robbery, Matchett was on probation for robbing a convenience store, and as part of that order was to avoid associating with Curtis.

Acting on the woman's tip, police visited Curtis' mother's home, where they found a plastic bag containing cash, jewellery and other items stolen from the Glendenning home. Hours later, the RCMP caught their biggest break of the investigation: a caller told investigators that Allan Legere was, at that very moment, sitting in a car pulled over on the side of the King George Highway in Newcastle, New Brunswick. Moments later, an officer located the car. Legere was sitting in the driver's seat.

Two weeks later, Matchett and Curtis emerged from a Toronto motel and surrendered to police. All three men were charged with second-degree murder. Although investigators didn't know which of the men had actually killed John Glendenning, under the Criminal Code of Canada, the fact that all three had been engaged in a robbery at the time made them equally culpable.

The trial for all three men was scheduled for January 1987, but the intervening months did not pass uneventfully. On November 17, 1986, Legere was playing cards with several inmates at the Dorchester Penitentiary when someone stabbed him in the back with a knife. Legere instinctively took off after Curtis, the knife still protruding from his back. The two ran into the rec room, throwing balls from a pool table at one another and fencing with pool cues. The altercation came to a halt only after a guard shoved his shotgun through a nearby port and ordered them to stop. Although the knife came within millimetres of his heart, Legere was discharged from hospital one week later. Curtis was subsequently charged with assault.

Despite the best efforts of Matchett's and Curtis' lawyers to have their clients tried separately from Legere, all three men were to be tried jointly in Newcastle by a jury. On January 7, the first day of the trial, Matchett suddenly informed Judge Paul Godin that he wanted to change his plea to guilty. Hours later, after Mary Glendenning had taken the stand, Curtis followed suit. Legere was the only one of the three to maintain his not guilty plea and go to trial.

Legere's lawyer, David Hughes, did not bother cross-examining Glendenning. There was little he could offer that would refute the testimony that followed. Donald Langan, a friend of Legere's, told the jury that the attack on the Glendenning home had been Legere's idea, and that the quartet had visited the home several times in the weeks leading up to the robbery. Legere's ex-girlfriend, Christine Searle, testified that Legere returned home around 4:00 AM the morning of the robbery and threw $15,000 on their bed. She said Legere maintained that Curtis and Matchett had been the ones to actually rob the Glendennings, and that all Legere had done was lend them his jacket. But the fact that Searle had later watched him burn a dollar bill with a "reddish-brown" stain on it convinced her otherwise.

Against Hughes' advice, Legere took the stand in his own defence. He confessed he had driven Curtis and Matchett to the Glendenning home on two previous occasions, but that he had spent the night of the robbery fixing his car. When Matchett and Curtis returned, they handed him a wad of cash, as well as the leather jacket Legere had loaned them.

It took the jury less than a day to come to their verdict. Legere, they announced, was guilty of second-degree murder. The sentence Justice Godin imposed was harsh: life in prison, with no possibility of parole for 18 years.

The verdict did not sit well with Legere. Approximately an hour and a half after being sentenced, while being transported to Moncton in a sheriff's car, Legere used a plastic fork to pick his handcuffs open and, when the car came to a stop, made a break for freedom. Fast as Legere was, the sheriff was faster, slamming Legere to the ground. He got Legere back into his cuffs, back into the car and completed the trip to Moncton without further incident.

He never told anyone about Legere's escape attempt. The information came out following Legere's next trial.

So four months later, two prison guards at the Atlantic Institution in Renous prepared Legere for the 90-minute drive to the hospital in Moncton for treatment of an ear infection, and neither knew of the incident. They both knew he was dangerous: a note in his file indicated he was to be kept under visual surveillance at all times. Legere, however, had been escorted to Moncton twice since his trial, for treatment of a recurring ear infection, and had never caused a problem. Regardless, Legere's legs were shackled, his hands cuffed to a belt wrapped around his waist. After the guards thoroughly strip-searched Legere, they piled into a van with Legere and a driver. It was 8:30 AM, on May 3, 1989.

Neither the guards nor the driver knew Legere had caused his own ear infection, repeatedly driving a pin into it. Even though Legere didn't smoke, neither guard thought much of Legere bringing two cigars into the van with him, one of which contained a makeshift key for his handcuffs. The guards had performed a full cavity search on Legere before they left the prison, but no one knew that he had jammed a TV antenna up his rectum.

Once inside the hospital, Legere asked if he could use the bathroom. He was shown to a single bathroom used mostly by hospital staff. One of the guards waited outside while the second started filling out Legere's forms. The door to the bathroom suddenly cracked open, and Legere spoke.

"I need some toilet paper."

A woman passing by the bathroom told him she'd get it. A heartbeat later, the door to the bathroom exploded open again, and Legere burst into the hallway, turned a corner and disappeared. His shackles, handcuffs and body belt lay in the bathroom sink.

One of the guards quickly gave chase, pursuing Legere down the hallway and out a nearby exit. The van driver saw Legere running up an embankment and started after him but backed off when the convict waved what turned out to be a TV antenna in his face. The guard who had followed Legere opened fire with the only weapon he had available, a can of Mace. Because the guards were not technically police officers, they weren't permitted to carry guns. The spray, however, deflected off Legere's back as he ran.

The last that any of the guards saw of Legere that day was when he hauled open the door of a car stopped at the gate to the hospital parking lot. He shoved the woman in the driver's seat over to one side, took the wheel and tore out of the parking lot. It was now 10:30 AM.

The guards quickly reported Legere's escape to the local police. Minutes later a woman named Peggy Olive called police to report she had been carjacked in the hospital parking lot. The man, who admitted to her he was escaping from jail, dropped her off at a nearby store. Her car was later found in the parking lot of a radio station in the city's west end. It was empty.

Allan Legere was gone.

The police in Chatham Head and neighbouring Newcastle knew Allan Legere very well.

He was born in 1948 to his mother, Louise, into a family of one older brother and two older sisters. Louise's first husband, Vince, described in the book *Terror's End: Allan Legere on Trial* as a "twisted, vicious" man, left Chatham Head in 1945 to find work and never came back. Louise took in boarders to help make ends meet. It was one of these boarders—Leonard Comeau—who had fathered Legere, then left.

Although Allan showed promise as a bright student early on, his attention span and behaviour quickly began a downward spiral. At the age of nine, his older brother, Freddy, was run over by a car while crossing a bridge with three friends. Police never charged the driver, and the Legeres developed a seething mistrust for the police that bordered on hatred.

When he started junior high school, Legere lifted weights three times a week to improve his physique. His body responded by growing increasingly strong but his brain did not. He failed the ninth grade and shortly afterwards embarked on a life of crime.

He was charged with theft, fined $15 and jailed for 15 days. Two years later, he served a 19-month sentence for theft over $50. He tried to work both as a lumberjack and a longshoreman, but nothing ever seemed to work out. At the age of 18, he married a psychiatric attendant with whom he fathered two children. He trained as a machinist and found work at a Nelson-Miramichi pulp mill. In 1972, he again found himself behind bars, jailed 14 months on three counts of possession of stolen property.

Although Legere would later deny it, *Terror's End* describes a steady descent into voyeurism, heavy drinking, drug use and an increasing fascination with both the Bible and the occult. He was a short-tempered, vicious man who acted on instinct, once beating a man who Legere believed had set fire to Louise's house. The man was later proven innocent.

On March 24, 1974, police picked Legere up for questioning during the course of a murder investigation. The body of Beatrice Redmond, 56, had been found in her Chatham Head home. The killing was particularly brutal: she had been stabbed 80 times. Despite police grilling him for 18 hours, Legere walked out of the police station a free man. The crime was never solved.

He took a job as the manager of the Zodiac Club in Chatham, a tough, seedy bar where Legere was just as likely to use his fists to settle disputes as any of his patrons. He lasted there until 1978 when a woman alleged that he had forced her into the DJ booth, tried to kiss her and pulled at her clothing. He spent 30 days in jail.

In 1979, Legere was again linked to a murder investigation. Nicholas Duguay was found murdered in his shack, hacked open by 67 axe blows. A jury found Robbie Cunningham, a friend of Legere's, guilty of manslaughter, believing Robbie was too stoned on LSD to understand the consequences of his actions.

Cunningham always maintained Legere had been responsible, a thesis backed up in the 1992 book *The Miramichi Axe Murder* by Sandra Mitchell.

Later in 1979, Legere ended up in prison again, this time serving a two-year sentence for stabbing a man in the face with a broken beer bottle. By now Legere's first marriage had ended and, despite stating he would never again take a wife, he married Donna Clouston O'Toole. The pair moved to Moncton in the summer of 1982 after he was paroled. Local police suddenly found themselves investigating a rash of burglaries. On August 19, police responded to a call from local resident Dr. Marcel Charlebois, who woke up to find a man inside his house. An officer later saw Legere emerging from the woods in the area around Charlebois' home, but when he gave chase, Legere bolted. Legere ran back to his trailer, where police surrounded him and called for him to give himself up. When he tried to sneak out a back window, one of the officers shot him in the shoulder, and Legere was caught. Police subsequently found several stolen items inside the home, including some jewellery reported missing from the Charlebois home.

His trial was scheduled to begin in August 1983. When the judge announced a four-day adjournment because two witnesses could not appear, Legere leaped to his feet and slashed his wrists with a hidden razor.

"That's what I think of this," he shouted, spraying blood all over the courtroom walls and floors.

The trial resumed two days later. Legere testified that he was jogging in the woods when he found a bunch of "junk jewellery," shortly before the police began chasing him. He announced he was planning to sue the city for damages as a result of being shot.

The jury didn't buy his story and returned a guilty verdict on one of two counts of breaking and entering. The judge sentenced Legere, who had already pleaded guilty to two counts of possession of stolen goods, to three years at the maximum-security prison in Dorchester, New Brunswick.

Authorities moved him to a medium-security prison, then back to the max because he kept picking fights with inmates. As his parole date grew closer, Donna Clouston O'Toole sold the car and trailer and fled the area.

"It would be very risky for me not to know he is free," Donna wrote to the parole board.

Upon his release, Legere proclaimed to anyone who would listen—usually the nearest police officer—that he had changed his ways. He lived with his mother and spent his days at the Fitness Warehouse gym in downtown Newcastle, sculpting his muscle-bound frame. In between his sets, Legere would cast appraising glances at two of the gym's female members: sisters Linda and Donna Daughney.

Within a year, Legere was back in jail, supposedly serving a life sentence for the murder of John Glendenning.

Now he was free.

As soon as they learned of Legere's escape, the local police set up roadblocks around Moncton, trying to limit his escape options. Search teams descended on the city's west end, where Legere had been known to operate before. Dog teams sniffed the area with their highly trained noses, and helicopters prowled the skies above the city, looking for him. Local papers played the story of his escape as front-page news, alerting the public to both Legere's newfound freedom and his violent past.

Within days, reports of sightings, thefts and attacks began dribbling in. On May 7, Max Ramsay, 62, was attacked by an unknown assailant while shoeing horses in a barn in Nova Scotia. The attacker took his wallet and car, both of which were found in the Miramichi River near Newcastle. On May 10, a woman who grew up with Legere told police she had just been settling into bed when she saw a man resembling Legere pop his head into her bedroom window. She crawled away and called police. She later discovered a necklace and a ring missing from her bedroom.

On May 27, Joe Ivory reported to police that someone had broken into his garage, stealing a duffel bag, a piece of pie and $100 worth of frozen meat.

Police responded to each sighting but still had no luck tracking down Legere. He was familiar with the area around Chatham Head and Newcastle, at home in the heavily forested banks of the Miramichi River. He had grown up and lived in the area, giving him a decided advantage in evading capture. Although some thought someone must be either harbouring or helping him, no one was ever able to prove it.

The reports, however, were little more than nuisance complaints, accounts of an escaped con stealing to survive. The investigation took a violent, sadistic turn during the early morning hours of May 29, 1989, when two police officers noticed flames shooting out of the Chatham home of sisters Annie and Nina Flam. Annie, 75, ran the small general store attached to the house where she lived with her widowed sister, Nina. The pair was well known in the community and loved by all of their patrons.

After radioing in for help from the fire department, the two officers rushed into the house, breaking down the back door. The pair found the burned but still-breathing body of Nina Flam at the bottom of a staircase and managed to get her out.

"Where's Annie?" they shouted. But Nina wasn't able to respond.

The first firefighters on scene made their way into the home, desperately trying to find Annie, but were forced back by the thick black smoke and overpowering heat of the blaze. When the rest of the fire department arrived on scene, crews attacked the fire and managed to save part of the house. Inside, buried under a pile of blackened rubble, they found the life-less body of Annie Flam.

Paramedics rushed Nina to Hôtel Dieu Hospital, where doctors fought to save her life. Forty percent of her body was covered in third-degree burns. Her pelvis and groin were badly bruised. When Nina told a nurse she'd been raped, doctors took three swabs from her vaginal area as part of a "rape kit."

When she began to recover, Nina told police that she and Annie had retired for the evening on May 28. Nina was sleeping lightly in her bedroom when a man wearing a mask appeared in her doorway. He held a knife to her throat, warned her to be quiet then tied her to the bed with pantyhose. He kept asking Nina where the money was, but Nina couldn't answer. He alternated between beating her and raping her, per-forming oral sex on her, then trying to force his penis into her mouth. He also called her "Mrs. Bernie," a reference to Nina's dead husband.

When he was finished, the man set fire to Nina's closet and her mattress, but not before cutting her free. When she tried to run out of the room, he pushed her back in. When she stumbled out into the hallway a second time, the man was gone.

Although police interviewed 60 suspects in the days following the grisly attack, they privately focused on Legere from the start. The more Nina talked, the more investigators recognized the violent mood swings and sexual aggression that were typical of

Legere's earlier crimes. They played a tape recording of his voice for Nina, but she didn't recognize it. All she could remember was that the man had light-coloured pubic hair.

The public also had its own ideas. Both Annie and Nina were considered treasures of the community, so the news of the murder and rape came as a shock to residents of Chatham Head and Newcastle. These same people who grieved Annie's death also knew Allan Legere. They had grown up with him, interacted with him and read about him in the newspaper. With each recounting of Annie's murder, Legere's name was inexorably linked to it.

The RCMP took over the investigation from the local police, publicly announcing that the description of Flam's attacker did not fit Legere.

On May 29, the Supreme Court of Canada issued a surprising and groundbreaking statement. Legere had appealed his conviction in the murder of John Glendenning to the country's highest judicial body, and at the time of his arrest, was waiting to hear whether or not the Court would hear the case. The justices announced that Legere had until the beginning of October to turn himself in if he wanted his appeal heard. No one could remember the court ever making such a declaration in the past.

On June 1, a man returning home with his wife saw a man trying to break into his garage. The homeowner took off after the man in his car but was forced to abandon the chase when the would-be burglar disappeared into the night. Days later, someone turned in a pair of glasses found near the scene of the chase to police. The style and prescription of the glasses matched those worn by Allan Legere while he was in prison.

With each new report and sighting, the communities lining the Miramichi grew increasingly fearful. They bought timers for their porch lights and bars for their windows, and dog breeders sold dogs in unheard-of numbers. Witnesses had placed Legere in Fredericton, Moncton and also in Toronto. By the end of July, however, the number of sightings dried up, and the people of New Brunswick thought that Legere had simply moved on.

Then on September 30, someone shot Morrisy Doran, 70, of Newcastle, in the back with a shotgun. The next day, someone armed with a shotgun broke into the home of Edwin Russell and his wife, Evangeline. The man took off after Edwin started to fight back. Police responded quickly to the report but could not find any trace of Legere.

Twelve days later, the Supreme Court announced it would not hear Legere's appeal.

On the morning of October 14, Danny Sullivan, a volunteer firefighter in Newcastle, was driving past the home of middle-aged sisters Linda and Donna Daughney when he saw smoke pouring out of the house. He quickly drove to the station, suited up and roared back to the home, calling in for help from the rest of the fire department and the police.

They found one body on the floor of a bedroom and quickly pulled her out of the burning house. A second body was found tucked into bed.

The two women were rushed to the nearby hospital but were both pronounced dead on arrival. Their bodies were so badly burned that the women could only be identified by their weight: Donna had been heavier than Linda.

The Daughney sisters had been living together since their father had passed away. Donna worked part time at the local welfare office and spent her lunch hours with Linda, who worked out at the Fitness Warehouse. Both were exceptionally friendly women, though Linda was remembered as being a little "slow." Both women were also fond of jewellery.

On the night before the fire, Linda had met a friend for coffee at Tim Hortons. She returned home at around 11:00 PM, according to witnesses. Police found a pool of blood near the back door, which was matched to Linda. They also discovered the back porch light had been unscrewed. Fire investigators determined that the fire had been deliberately set. One of the bedroom closets showed signs of having been lit, but the fire had not taken. The attacker had most likely left and returned to start a second blaze.

Autopsies showed that both sisters had been raped. Linda's jaw was broken in several places. Donna had a broken nose and jaw, five broken ribs and a ruptured blood vessel in her brain. There was a puncture wound in her throat. She had choked on her own vomit and died. Linda had died as a result of the fire.

Investigators were determined to keep a close lid on the attack, only releasing that both women had been beaten and sexually assaulted. They admitted that Legere was a suspect but one of possibly many. Still, the sense of security that had blossomed in Newcastle since July was quickly shattered by news of the attack. The similarities between the Daughneys' murders and Annie Flam's murder could not be ignored. All three women had been sexually assaulted, and both homes had been set on fire.

The less the police talked, the more fearful the community became. Fathers and husbands slept either on the living room couch or kept loaded weapons within arm's reach of their beds. Families operated on a schedule, with children reporting in to parents at specific times. Many communities cancelled Halloween, instead hosting parties at community halls. At public meetings, frustrated residents openly declared what they would do if someone broke into their homes.

"There's no jury in the world that's going to convict you for shooting scum like that," one shouted.

The local Crime Stoppers chapter offered a reward for information leading to the arrest of the suspects in the Flam and Daughney murders. The reward started at $2000, climbed to $10,000 and then to $30,000. Within a month, the group was offering $50,000.

Two weeks later, the police held a news conference saying there was no evidence linking Legere to the Daughney murders but then issued a press release cancelling all further news conferences. The media and the public were enraged by the decision, but there was little anyone could do about it.

The following day, one officer in Newcastle had a close call with a suspect who had just stolen two guns from a truck parked at the Morada Motel. He had received a call from a resident who had seen a man pass his window, point a gun at him and tell him to go back to sleep. The officer's dog picked up a scent and tracked the suspect into the woods. Although he repeatedly came within just a few metres of the suspect, the officer was forced back each time by wild shotgun fire. He called in for backup near the Miramichi Golf and Country Club, but by the time help arrived, the man had disappeared. The only thing the police would say to the public was that a shot had been fired at the golf course.

After being publicly beaten by the media for several days over their secret approach to the investigation, the police finally held another news conference, informing the public that all officers' annual leave had been cancelled; that they had interviewed 50 suspects; and that there were nearly 100 officers working on the streets. They were doing all they could.

Investigators, however, had caught a forensic break. Since the attack on the Flam sisters in May, police had been waiting for the RCMP laboratory in Ottawa to install the proper equipment necessary to conduct DNA testing. The "genetic fingerprinting" technique was a new investigative tool in the police arsenal that was only just being utilized in North America. The process takes samples of fluid from a suspect and, using a chemical process, breaks up the DNA double helix that serves as the building block in all life. After exposing the genetic material to electricity and radioactive chemicals, then x-raying, police can match the fluid sample to a particular person's genetic makeup. Because each person carries a unique DNA sequence, police can, on the basis of DNA evidence, place a person at a crime scene without any witnesses.

The process was still being heavily criticized by some scientists in the U.S. but was already proving useful in Canada. The investigation in the Miramichi, however, was to be DNA's coming-out party.

Police announced that they had matched genetic material found at the Flam crime scene with material collected in the Daughney murders—both crimes were committed by the same person. They named Allan Legere as a suspect but did not name anyone else.

On November 15, police announced they had arrested Allard Vienneau, 30, in the attacks on Morrissy Doran, and Edwin and Evangeline Russell.

The following day, a group of parishioners began arriving at the Church of the Blessed Virgin Mary in Chatham Head for an evening mass. The lights in the parish were off. By 7:10 PM, the group of worshipers grew nervous. No one had yet seen Father James Smith.

Nick Verriker, a parishioner who helped Father Smith around the church grounds, used his key to check the rest of the building. When he entered the rectory, he found the kitchen in shambles, pools of blood congealing on the floor. Police later found Father Smith's body in his study. His face had been slashed by a knife. His entire rib cage had been caved in. Father Smith, like Donna Daughney, had died choking on his own vomit.

From the analysis of the crime scene and the body, police determined Smith had been killed at some point in the early morning hours of November 16, yet his attacker had waited until the evening hours to actually leave. Smith's 1984 Oldsmobile 88 Delta was missing from the garage. Inside the rectory, investigators found a church bulletin lying on the floor, with a bloodstained boot print on it.

Police in Bathurst called in at approximately 10:00 PM saying they had located Father Smith's car at the local train station. A ticket attendant confirmed that earlier that night he had sold a ticket to Montréal to a man roughly matching Legere's description. Alerted by their counterparts in New Brunswick, Québec police boarded the train at Levis and searched all the passengers. They came across a man sleeping in his seat, who gave his name as Fernand Savoie.

Québec police were told to look for a man with two tattoos—one of an eagle head and a star on his right forearm and a second of an eagle on his right bicep. When the police on the train asked Savoie to roll up his sleeve, they did not see any tattoo on his forearm and moved on.

They didn't bother checking the man's left forearm, which was where Legere's tattoo actually was.

A frightened public was now sleeping, eating and working on a razor's edge, waiting for the killer to strike again. Officers in cars and on foot patrolled the streets while members of the RCMP's provincial Emergency Response Team (ERT) prowled the area in their distinctive black uniforms, carrying automatic weapons. Although winter was coming, ERT teams descended into the wilderness of the Miramichi, setting up camps and sleeping in the woods. Some residents called for the federal government to send in the military. The RCMP responded by saying that they didn't need more bodies, they needed more information.

Days passed with no new attacks and no new information. On November 23, a snowstorm blew into New Brunswick, blanketing the entire province in thunderous winds and thick snowfall. At approximately 2:00 AM, a call went out to all New Brunswick RCMP officers on duty. Legere was at a gas station near Sussex. An off-duty RCMP officer named Michelle Mercer had stopped to pick up a taxi driver and a passenger who were stranded on the side of the road. Within minutes of Mercer pulling away from the side of the highway, the passenger pulled a gun on Mercer and ordered her to drive to Moncton.

"Please do as I say. I'm the one they're looking for. I'm Allan Legere."

When Mercer told Legere that she needed to stop for gas, he agreed. Mercer pulled into a Sussex gas station, where Legere took the car keys from the ignition and went out to pump gas. When he walked into the store to pay for the fuel, Mercer quickly grabbed her spare set of car keys and drove herself and the taxi driver to the Sussex RCMP station.

Officers who arrived at the gas station could not find Legere. The call went out across the province; police set up roadblocks on every major highway, searching every car that passed. They had caught a break that they prayed would pan out.

At approximately 5:00 AM, police received a call from a trucker out on the road. The trucker had seen a semi-trailer travelling without its load on a highway not typically used by heavy trucks. Corporals Terry Barter and Gary Lutwick, manning a nearby roadblock, sped off to the area and located the truck. When they flipped on their overhead lights, however, the truck at first refused to pull over. Half a kilometre later it did.

Lutwick pulled his service pistol from his holster, while Barter trained his M-16 automatic rifle on the truck. The driver's door opened and a frightened, wild-eyed Brian Golding tumbled out into the road.

"It's him. He's got a gun!" Golding shouted.

After searching Golding, both officers moved in on the truck, approaching it from opposite sides, shouting commands. A hand appeared in the window and moments later a gun landed in the snow at the officers' feet. The door then cracked open, and a thin, dark-haired man stepped out of the cab.

"I'm Allan Legere," he said, just as the officers moved in and threw him to the ground.

After seven months at large, the Monster of Miramichi was now in custody.

August 26, 1991

Security at Oromocto High School, 8 kilometres outside of Fredericton, New Brunswick, had never been so tight.

The province had sent 510 letters to prospective jurors to decide the guilt or innocence of Allan Legere on four counts of first-degree murder, but only 180 prospective jurors showed up for selection at the high school. Under the watchful eye of Court of Queen's Bench Justice David Dickson, defence attorney Weldon Furlotte and lead Crown counsel Tony Allman questioned each potential juror. After two days, the jury was selected. Six men and six women would hear the case, which would begin the next day at the Burton courthouse outside Fredericton.

The police had taken their time compiling the evidence against Legere, waiting almost a year to formally charge him. In the time between his arrest and his trial, Legere had already been found guilty of escaping lawful custody and kidnapping Peggy Olive and sentenced to nine years in prison.

Furlotte had a difficult time organizing his defence. Dickson was determined to get the trail going quickly, denying Furlotte's motion months earlier for a time extension to better prepare. Furlotte got permission to hire a second attorney, but his choice, Bill Kearney, had been far from stellar. Kearney had been fired from his previous job for a series of sexual indiscretions involving young girls. Also, Kearney and Legere never got along, and just two weeks into the trial, Legere fired him.

The Crown's case was far from a slam-dunk either. They had no concrete witness statements placing Legere at the scene of any of the murders. What they had, Allman explained to the jury, was a litany of circumstantial evidence backed up by the new science of DNA matching that pointed to Legere as the killer in all four cases. Furlotte explained he would refute the DNA testing with expert testimony that the DNA of the people of the Miramichi region was so inbred that it would be remarkably similar to anyone else who lived in the area.

Legere took an active role in his own defence, even though he spent every day in court shackled to a post in the courtroom floor. He repeatedly stood up and interrupted the court, accusing the jury of being prejudiced, accusing Dickson of acting against him and generally being a nuisance. On several occasions,

Dickson ordered Legere removed from the court-room. A closed circuit TV camera was set up in the courtroom, and Legere watched the proceedings from his cell. On each occasion, Dickson allowed Legere back in court, only after he had apologized.

The Crown called 243 witnesses while presenting its case to the jury. Nina Flam recounted the horror of her sexual assault at her attacker's hands. At one point, Furlotte asked the court if Dickson would per-mit Legere to pull down his pants to show Flam his pubic hair, as that was the only part of her attacker that Flam had seen. Dickson angrily denied the request.

A Montréal pawnbroker testified that a man named Fernand Savoie had come to his store and sold him several pieces of jewellery, which police were able to link to the Daughney sisters. The pawnbroker, how-ever, could not identify Legere in the courtroom. Staff from the Montréal hotel where Savoie had stayed testified about a man who had stayed there for sev-eral days in November 1989, seldom leaving his room. Two gym rats from the Fitness Warehouse recounted lewd comments Legere had made about Donna Daughney.

As the trial wound towards October, Dickson sur-prised reporters and onlookers alike when he dismissed Jeff Moorcraft from the jury. Since late September Moorcraft had been associating with Pamela Kellar before and after court. When Kellar attended court, she sat with Caroline Norwood and Lois Gaunce, two women who were convinced of Legere's innocence. Norwood later left her husband because Legere proposed to her. The wedding never happened.

Police began following Kellar, sitting close by and eavesdropping on conversations she had with Norwood and Gaunce. On one occasion, when discussing the case, Kellar said that Legere "had someone going for him." When police brought their findings to Dickson, he quickly dismissed Moorcraft from duty and ordered the trial to continue.

A string of RCMP investigators took the stand. One officer who interviewed Legere after his arrest told the court about a series of camps along the Miramichi that Legere had lived in during his time at large. RCMP Sergeant Robert Kennedy showed the jury how he had matched Legere's feet to a pair of boots found outside the Bathurst train station, and how he also determined those same boots had left the print on the church bulletin in Father Smith's rectory. Dr. John Brown, head of the RCMP lab in Ottawa, gave jurors a crash course in DNA and how he had matched material from Annie Flam and the Daughneys to Legere. In the case of Donna, there was a 1-in-7400 chance the DNA belonged to Legere. In Nina's case, the odds were 1 in 5.2 million. Those odds exploded in Linda's case. There was a 1-in-310-million chance that the DNA material recovered belonged to someone other than Allan Legere.

The Crown also brought in Dr. Kenneth Kidd from Yale University to refute the defence claim that the

Miramichi area was so inbred that proper DNA test-ing was impossible. Kidd described DNA research conducted on centuries-old South American tribes in which no new genetic material had entered their gene pool for hundreds, even thousands of years. In those cases, Kidd said, experts were able to distin-guish each member's DNA from the rest of the tribe. The Miramichi, said Kidd, was not that isolated.

Furlotte called only one witness in Legere's defence. Dr. William Shields from State University in New York was supposed to confirm his in-breeding theory. Shields instead testified that he agreed with the RCMP testing in the case, though he said that the odds Allan Legere was responsible for Linda Daughney's murder were closer to 1 in 11 million rather than 1 in 310 mil-lion. When one looked at Canada's population at the time of the murder and eliminated half that number to account for the female population, then several mil-lion more to account for those too young or old to commit the murder, Shields admitted there were less than 10 million Canadians who could have committed the murder. His 1-in-11-million estimate of Legere's DNA match meant Legere was effectively the only Canadian who could have committed the murders.

Furlotte announced he was finished presenting his defence. He refused to put Legere on the stand. Instead, Furlotte tried to rally his closing remarks around his theory on in-breeding, even though his one and only witness had done little to bolster the argument.

"If Allan Legere is wrongfully convicted today, it could be you or a loved one tomorrow. If you have any doubt whatsoever, you must acquit," Furlotte said.

Allman weaved together his own story one last time, threading together the circumstantial evidence and DNA testing to buttress his argument that Allan Legere was guilty. On November 2, Dickson charged the jury, who went into deliberations shortly after 3:00 PM. Dickson had also taken the unusual step of ordering the jury sequestered during the trial because of the level of publicity the trial received.

Two days later, the jury reached a verdict. When the court reconvened, Legere at first refused to come out of his cell. After 10 minutes of coaxing and cajoling, Legere finally entered the prisoner's box. The jury filed in and declared Legere guilty in each of the four counts of first-degree murder.

As quickly as the jury had come to their verdict, Dickson was even faster in imposing Legere's sentence. On each count, Dickson sentenced Legere to life in jail with no possibility of parole for 25 years, the maximum allowed under the Criminal Code of Canada.

"This trial's not done yet Your Honour," Legere said as he was led away. "We'll have round number two."

After Legere left the courtroom, Dickson responded to the jury, "...I will say this: don't lose too much sleep over your verdict."

Although Furlotte immediately announced he would appeal the verdict the following day, his declaration was lost in the wave of celebration that washed over New Brunswick. Few doubted that Legere was responsible from the start. He had terrified a region of 50,000 people for seven months, sparked a manhunt that cost the federal and provincial governments close to $1 million and had killed four innocent people.

Legere did not fade quietly from the public mindset. On December 13, 1991, corrections authorities ordered Legere transferred from the Atlantic Institution to the Special Hand Unit (SHU) at Sainte-Anne-des-Plaines prison in Montréal after corrections officers received a tip that he was planning to take a female guard hostage and try to escape. In 1994, Legere announced he was suing the staff at the SHU because he kept getting beaten up.

The Miramichi, however, tried its best to forget Allan Legere. In 1995, the towns of Chatham and Newcastle united with three surrounding villages to become the city of Miramichi. A seniors' home in the city was christened Father Smith Manor, and a world globe, in memory of Annie Flam, was purchased for the library.

As of the writing of this book, Legere is still being held at the SHU outside Montréal. He will be eligible for parole in 2014.

CHAPTER THREE

Paul Bernardo
(1964–)
Karla Homolka
(1970–)

July 2005

DOZENS OF REPORTERS, PHOTOGRAPHERS AND CAMERA CREWS had been camped outside a Montréal prison for days, waiting for Canada's most despised, most hated woman to show her face outside the prison walls. Only weeks earlier, a judge had ignored the arguments of her lawyer that she had already paid her debt to society and ordered that the woman, now 35, continue to observe a series of conditions usually imposed on convicted felons serving probationary terms. She had to provide a DNA sample, not contact the families of her victims, have no contact with any criminals and inform the police if she changed her name, address, job or appearance.

Beginning in 1993 with the arrest of her husband on charges of first-degree murder and sexual assault, there were few faces in Canada as well known and reviled as that of Karla Homolka's.

And yet, when her lawyers drove her out of the Sainte-Anne-des-Plaines penitentiary in Québec, the few dozen waiting reporters who had been closely scrutinizing every vehicle that entered and left the institution completely missed hers.

The reporters' first clue that she had been released came two hours later when Karla Homolka, aka Karla Bernardo, aka Karla Leanne Teale, walked into RDI TV station in Montréal and, in slightly accented but fluent French, asked the public to leave her alone.

"I don't want to be hunted down. I don't want people to think I am dangerous and I'm going to do something to their children," she said.

She tiptoed around the issue of her involvement in the killings of three Ontario teenagers, one of whom had been her younger sister. Homolka refused to answer questions about her rumoured romantic relationship with convicted killer Jean-Paul Gerbet. She wouldn't answer questions about where she was going to live and what she was going to do.

She had served her 12-year sentence on two counts of manslaughter, Homolka told the reporter who tried to question her. She had lived every day with the pain, guilt and shame of knowing she had been a party to three of the most grisly, sensationalized murders in Canada.

Now that she was a free woman, Karla Homolka told the world what she really craved was refreshment.

"This is stupid. I'd like to have an iced cappuccino. An iced cappuccino from Tim Hortons, that's what I'd like to do."

Minutes later, a perfectly coiffed Karla Leanne Teale, known to the rest of the country as Karla Homolka, former wife of a convicted schoolgirl killer, left the television station and tried to disappear.

Reporters were able to track her down at her new job at a hardware store in Longueuil on Montréal's south shore. Her boss, Richer Lapointe, later confirmed the location for the media and also shared with them several audio tapes of his and Homolka's conversations, talking about how she had violated the conditions of her release. When the story broke, Homolka disappeared from view. It was later revealed that Lapointe himself had recently been charged with sexual assault by his wife. Shortly afterwards, Rona decided to shut down the store.

In June 2006, a Québec court refused to hear Homolka's latest appeal to change her name. She now wanted to be known to the world as Emily Chiara Tremblay, one of the most common surnames in Québec. However, the judge ruled that her current name, which had been changed to Karla Leanne Teale before her husband's 1994 trial, was not that well known across the country and therefore refused her request.

Few Canadians may know who Karla Leanne Teale is, but every parent knows the name of Karla Homolka. They also know the name of her former husband Paul Bernardo and know that the "Ken and Barbie" couple from St. Catharines jointly participated in one of the most sadistic crimes ever committed in Canada's history.

And almost every moment had been caught on
film.

Located on Ontario's Welland Canal, Lake Gibson
does not ebb and flow with the lunar cycle. The lake is
a critical component of Ontario Hydro's power grid,
and its water level rises and falls with the demand for
power in the area.

On the evening of June 29, 1991, the water level of
the lake was more shallow than usual, but that didn't
stop small groups of boaters and fishers from enjoying
the cool summer night out on the water. Bill and
Linda Grekul skilfully piloted their canoe across the
glassy surface. Bill's thoughts, however, kept drifting
back to the strange concrete block he had seen on the
lake's shoreline.

Some movement on land caught his eye, and Bill
spotted fisherman Mike Doucette working his way
along the waterline, towards the mysterious block.
Bill waved and hollered at Doucette, imploring him to
have a closer look at the foreign object.

Within minutes, Doucette was on the phone to the
police. What he'd seen inside the cement block was
a sight he wouldn't soon be able to erase from his
mind. Even though the flesh had mixed with the concrete, Doucette knew he was looking at a small cluster
of human body parts encased in cement.

Doucette's grisly find was just one of the six the
police would uncover over the next 24 hours. As they

patrolled the shoreline, officers from the Niagara Regional Police Department pulled four more blocks from Lake Gibson. Each cement brick contained another horrifying assortment of human remains: feet mixed with arms, and hands with legs. One block alone contained the disembodied head of what appeared to be a young girl.

Had the water level of the lake risen, no one would have found the remains for several days, if ever. Photographers and forensic identification technicians swarmed over the lake, snapping photos and recovering evidence. Ontario Hydro lowered the lake's water level further so that the police could continue their search, but no more concrete blocks were found. They had recovered the human remains of one person, most likely a female, all except for the torso. Despite their best efforts, they could find no seventh block that might contain it.

The next day, the police received another frantic phone call. A fisherman who had been turned away from Lake Gibson because of the investigation and told to try his luck at the nearby Faywell bridge had spotted what looked like human remains floating under the bridge. He was holding in place with his fishing rod what turned out to be the missing torso. He sent his friends to call the police.

All of the remains were transferred to Hamilton General Hospital, where the concrete blocks were broken apart. Although the nature of the evidence already spoke to the facts, closer inspection of the unknown person's remains proved the individual "now classified as a female" had been deliberately dismembered. The cuts through bone and the torn flesh made it clear that someone had used a power saw on the poor girl's body after she was dead. The police scoured the body and its seven separate cement tombs for clues to the woman's identity, but they came up with little. They knew she had brown eyes, and they knew she had braces. Despite a thorough autopsy on what remained, no cause of death could be conclusively determined. The remains were eventually locked away until they could be claimed, but the medical examiner who conducted the autopsy refused to sign off on the final report.

The find was one of the most gut wrenching in Ontario's history. Few of the officers who started working the case could fathom how anyone could inflict that kind of damage on another human being.

Just 50 kilometres away on Niagara-on-the-Lake, on the exact same day the police had first found the cement blocks, a young St. Catharines couple was celebrating their marriage with 400 of their closest friends and family.

During the week previous, members of the Niagara Regional Police Department had tried to identify the young girl. No brown-eyed girls were reported missing who matched the age range of their victim, so the police used what distinguishing features they had—namely the girl's braces—and obtained the names of four girls recently reported to Child Find as missing.

The medical examiner had to look only briefly at the dental charts in order to match the braces on the dismembered head to those worn by Burlington teenager Leslie Mahaffy.

Leslie's parents had reported her missing on June 14, just two weeks before she was to turn 15. The strong-willed, fiercely independent brunette had proven quite the ordeal for her parents over the last several months: smoking, being caught shoplifting and even running away from home. Although Leslie eventually returned home, her parents Dan and Debbie had imposed a set of strict rules on their wayward daughter. She had to observe a strict curfew, could not have her own house key and had to attend all of her high school classes. She had not quite settled down, though the Mahaffys felt Leslie was finally starting to come around.

On the night of June 14, Leslie and a group of students attended a wake for a friend who had recently been killed in a single-vehicle accident. The group stood around at The Rock, a local hangout, and drank beer, remembering their friend. Leslie's parents had given her permission to stay out past her 11:00 PM curfew so long as she called and told them when she would be home.

Mahaffy never called.

By interviewing her friends, the police learned that one of them had dropped Leslie off at her home around 1:00 AM, well past her curfew. Minutes later, Leslie phoned another friend, Amanda Carpino, from the pay phone of a nearby convenience store. Leslie told her friend that her house was locked, and she didn't have a key. She asked if she could spend the night at Amanda's. Amanda said she didn't think it was a good idea because it was so late. The two girls chatted for a few moments, then Leslie promised Amanda they'd talk after the funeral for their friend, which was scheduled for the next day.

Leslie never made it to the funeral. When Debbie Mahaffy woke up the next day, she couldn't find Leslie anywhere. Both she and Dan called Leslie's friends, trying to find out what had happened to her. By the time the sun went down, the Mahaffys were frantic: even when Leslie had run away before, she had phoned them almost every day to let them know she was all right. They had not heard from her in almost a day.

The Mahaffys called the police, who knew about Leslie's past and were inclined to treat the teenager's disappearance as a runaway. As the days passed, however, and still no one had heard from Leslie, the police began to take the case more seriously. When Mahaffy's remains were finally identified almost a month later on July 9, the police knew they were dealing with one of the most serious crimes in their history.

On July 10, the police informed the Mahaffys that the remains found in Lake Gibson were, in fact, those of their daughter. Although Leslie had blue eyes, the medical examiner surmised that the lime content of the concrete had leached the colour from the young girl's eyes after she'd died, leaving them a lifeless, soulless brown.

July 10 was also Debbie Mahaffy's birthday.

Members of the sexual assault squad in Toronto were growing increasingly confused.

The squad had been formed in response to a series of violent rapes that had been taking place in one of Toronto's suburbs since the late 1980s. Dubbed "The Scarborough Rapist," the man had groped or raped 14 women.

The Scarborough Rapist was the sexual assault squad's raison d'être. The division of the Toronto Metropolitan police had been formed in response to the rapist's growing number of attacks. The pattern was always the same. All the rapes took place in Scarborough, and they took place late at night. Almost all of the women were attacked minutes after stepping off a bus. During the first couple of rapes, the attacker had done little more than grope his victims. But soon afterwards, the violence of the attacks escalated sharply. He blitzed his victims from behind, holding a knife to their throats and forcing them into dark areas in between other houses. He never let his victims look at him, threatening them with death if they tried to catch a glimpse of his face. He forced them to perform oral sex on him then raped them vaginally or anally. On at least one occasion, after telling his victim to lie still for a specified number of minutes, the attacker returned and raped her again. He made his victims talk to him while he assaulted them. In one instance, he continually told one of the women to wish his penis a Merry Christmas.

Only two women had gotten a good look at their attacker. The first such attack took place in Mississauga, and the victim was able to provide a detailed description to a police sketch artist. The composite drawing was never made public. A second sketch divined from the details obtained by a Scarborough victim, however, was eventually released to the press on May 29, 1990. The police had no suspects and, despite their best efforts, also had no luck in trying to catch the guy in the act.

No sooner had the first newspapers containing the sketch hit the streets than the phones at the sexual assault squad's offices started ringing off the hook. The sketch seemed to look like everyone's ex-boyfriend, ex-husband or co-worker. The publicity of the attacks, coupled with the $150,000 reward, guaranteed a large volume of calls, "16,000 in total"—so much so that members of the squad could not possibly investigate all of them.

A month later on June 28, a teller at a Royal Bank in Toronto called the squad and told the receptionist that the composite closely resembled one of her customers, a man named Paul Bernardo. She had not seen Mr. Bernardo for almost a month. Her report was filed away with hundreds of others.

Bernardo's name, however, came up again three months later when a woman called the squad and also said the man in the sketch closely resembled Paul. Two weeks after this call, the woman, named Tina, and her husband Alex Smirnis, showed up at the detachment for an interview. Alex, it turned out, had a brother, Van, who had been a close friend of Bernardo's since childhood. The couple turned over photos of the man who closely resembled the sketch. Alex even hinted to investigators that he knew Bernardo had been responsible for at least one rape in his lifetime.

While investigating the Smirnis' allegations, Constable Steve Irwin came across a report from a previous rape by the Scarborough Rapist that had been somehow misfiled. The report, detailing the assault of a woman who had gotten a good look at her attacker's face, also contained a supplementary report by a Toronto Island officer, Sergeant Kevin McNiff. In the report, McNiff discussed the alleged assault by Paul Bernardo of his former girlfriend Jennifer Galligan. According to Galligan (who had come to McNiff not to press charges but to get back some money Bernardo owed her), the couple had last been together on the night of November 19, after Paul's graduation from university. According to Galligan, the pair went out for drinks, where Bernardo criticized her in public, complaining about the gifts she got him and insinuating she slept with other men. When they got in the car later that night, Bernardo started beating her. He drove her to an abandoned parking lot and pulled out a knife, saying that he was going to rape her. Galligan bolted, running away from Bernardo's white Capri and disappearing into a nearby ravine.

One of the Scarborough victims had mentioned she thought the rapist drove a white Capri, the same make and model that Bernardo drove. Between the newly found report, the Smirnis' complaint, the car and the likeness between Bernardo and the composite sketch, Irwin and his partner John Munroe decided they had more than enough reason to justify sitting down with this Paul Bernardo.

∙❖∙

As Stephen Williams wrote in his book, *Invisible Darkness: The Strange Case of Paul Bernardo and Karla Homolka*, "The one guy who was always nice to Karla, who never bored her—whom she knew from the moment they met she would marry—was born a bastard on August 27, 1964 at Scarborough General Hospital in the suburbs of Toronto. He had also been very ugly."

Paul had been conceived illegitimately, outside the sacred vows between his mother, Marilyn Bernardo (née Hamilton) and her husband, Ken Bernardo. Tired of Ken's beatings, Marilyn had found refuge in the arms of her former suitor, a man named Bill—a man her father had refused to let her marry. The result of their tryst was Paul, born with a large blood clot on his face that faded weeks after his birth.

Despite knowing of Paul's lineage, Ken still gave the boy his last name and tried to raise him with the rest of the Bernardo family. Paul's upbringing, however, was not an easy one. He did not speak a word for two years because his tongue was fused to his palate. Once the problem was rectified, Paul began to speak and grow like any other boy, despite his surroundings. His mother dove into a wallowing depression that isolated her from the rest of the world. She lived in her bedroom and put on a grotesque amount of weight. When Ken wasn't ridiculing her, he was peeping into the bedrooms of women in their neighbourhood or sexually assaulting Paul's sister, Debbie.

One night when Paul was a teenager, he and his mother got into a fight. Marilyn threw a photo down on his bed and explained that the man in the photo was, in fact, Paul's father. The exchange became typical of their relationship. Marilyn called Paul a "b*****d from hell" to his face, while Bernardo responded by calling her a cow. Nevertheless, Paul was doing well in life. He was a Queen's Scout, studied judo and worked in a restaurant. He was later accepted to the University of Toronto to study accounting and, upon graduating, landed a job with the prestigious accounting firm of Price Waterhouse.

Bernardo's success, however, was merely a thin veneer that barely contained the growing animal within. Paul enjoyed sex—the rougher the better. Bernardo had been dating Jennifer Galligan for three years, but he cheated on her regularly while constantly foisting kinkier, more violent sex on her. He developed a liking for anal sex. He also beat Jennifer repeatedly. During the time they dated, the police had responded to at least two calls about incidents between the pair.

Irwin and Munroe could not believe for a second that the man they were talking to could be a rapist.

The two detectives had made the trip to Ken Bernardo's home on Sir Raymond Drive on November 19, but Paul had not been home. He did respond to their message, however, and met the detectives at their downtown offices for an interview later that afternoon. Bernardo was charming, laid-back and witty, explaining to the officers that his likeness to the composite sketch released to the media had been noted by more than one person. He did not find it funny at all, he said. He would never treat a woman that way. He told Irwin and Munroe he was currently unemployed, was in love with a veterinarian's assistant who lived in St. Catharines and that he was planning on marrying her and moving out to the city to be with her.

The detectives interviewed Bernardo for less than an hour before scrubbing him from their list of suspects. They did ask him to provide blood, saliva and hair samples, which he did willingly. Bernardo shook their hands on the way out the door, wishing them luck.

Although neither officer suspected Bernardo as the Scarborough Rapist, the move to get blood, saliva and hair samples from him was ultimately geared towards making their job easier. The Centre for Forensic Sciences had successfully isolated a stain found on the panties of one of the victims. Using the stain, technicians were able to determine a unique fact about the assailant: he was a "non-secretor," meaning that his blood type could not be divined through his saliva. Non-secretors make up only 20 percent of the population, which helped narrow down the range of possible suspects. They also knew the attacker was white, which further honed the focus of their investigation. The technicians at the lab were excited: once they had a sample to compare against the stain, they could try to match the two by comparing their DNA.

DNA testing, however was still a relatively new science in Canada. It first made its splash during the Allan Legere murder trial in 1991, but few scientists in Canada were sufficiently qualified to conduct the testing. Most testing in Canadian cases was done in the United States and took up to three months to complete.

Still, staff at the Centre for Forensic Sciences were optimistic. Kim Johnston, a scientist at the centre, instructed the police to separate their suspects using the non-secretor status as a guide. Therefore, the police were eventually able to isolate 21 suspects who fit the appropriate age, race and non-secretor status identified in the investigation. Johnston also told Irwin to get blood samples from all 21 suspects, which could then be analyzed using conventional serology (blood-typing). Once the suspects whose blood type did not match the type found in the panty stain were weeded out, the lab would perform DNA testing on the remaining six or so samples.

Starting in 1990, with each new suspect they investigated, the police tried to obtain new blood samples. In total, Irwin and his squad submitted over 130 samples to the Centre for Forensic Sciences for a serology workup. The process, however, was time consuming. By 1990 the rapes had stopped, and the importance of the investigation began to wane.

Serial killers or rapists only stop killing or raping for one of three reasons: they die, they are incarcerated for an unrelated offence or they move away from their usual hunting grounds. Most of those who do move continue to kill or rape once they become familiar with their new locale.

In the winter of 1990, Paul Bernardo moved out of his parents' Scarborough home and into the home of his fiancée's family. His fiancée was Karla Homolka.

Karla Homolka was born in Mississauga, Ontario, on May 4, 1970, to Karel and Dorothy Homolka (née Seger). Karel was born in Czechoslovakia before immigrating to Canada with his family at the age of seven. Dorothy was Ontario born and bred. The pair met in Mississauga and married in 1965. While Dorothy worked as a secretary at the Lakeshore Psychiatric Centre, Karel stumbled through a series of meaningless jobs, from selling trinkets outside shopping malls to being a travelling salesman. Karla was not the only child in their family. There were three daughters in the Homolka clan: Karla, Lori, and Tammy Lyn, the youngest of the three.

Karla may very well have been the smartest of her sisters. When tested in school, she scored 131 on an IQ test, significantly above average for her age. From the time she was a child, Karla seemed to know just how smart she was. She charmed her schoolmates with relative ease, recruiting friends into her inner circle. She loved animals so much that she attended Grade 12 only part time so she could work full time at a pet store. In her teens she used drugs and drank alcohol. Ever the braggart, she openly told her father to "f**k off" or called him a "dumb Czech."

She recruited a group of girlfriends into "The Diamond Club," its sole reason for existence was for the women to marry wealthy men who would buy them large engagement rings. Homolka also dabbled in the occult. She played with Ouija boards, dressed all in black and wore thick mascara. One summer, she saved up all her money and, without telling her parents, flew to Kansas City to spend a week with a former boyfriend who had moved there earlier in the year.

In October 1987, however, another trip was going to be even more fantastic for Karla Homolka. She was going to the big city—Toronto—with her boss and another co-worker to attend a pet expo. Normally only her boss went to these events, but this year she had invited Karla and Debbie Purdie to go with her. Karla and Debbie were determined to have a good time and to party. But their boss, Kristy, had other ideas and was determined to safeguard her employees. She kicked out the first pair of guys that the two girls brought back to the hotel room. Exasperated,

Debbie and Karla decided to grab a late dinner at Bluffer's Atrium Lounge.

Within minutes of their arrival, a cute guy began chatting them up. He introduced himself as Paul and told them he was an accountant in Toronto. He also introduced his lifelong friend, Van Smirnis, to Debbie.

The connection was instantaneous. Within an hour Karla invited the men back to her and Debbie's hotel room. And within another hour, Paul and Karla were having sex.

From that moment on, their relationship blossomed. Karla fell hard for the attractive, young accountant, declaring early on to her friends and family that she had met the man she was going to marry. Paul took her to the Price Waterhouse Christmas party, introducing her to all of his co-workers. In the spring, Paul escorted Karla to her high school graduation. It was at this point, however, that his jealous side started to show. When Karla started talking with some of her male friends at her graduation party, Paul picked a fight with them. The police were called to the scene, but no charges were ever laid.

The foundation of their relationship lay in their sex lives. In Karla, Paul had found a woman willing to satisfy his most erotic desires, even when those desires grew more and more sinister. She introduced a pair of handcuffs into their ritual, letting Paul bind her and ravage her. They also started using gags. Paul took Polaroid photos of Karla naked and videotaped her with a home camcorder he had purchased. Karla took to calling his penis "Snuffles" and wrote Paul an endless stream of love notes and cards, stating exactly what she wanted him to do to her.

In December 1989, things in Karla's life seemed to come together. She got a job with the Martindale Vet Clinic in St. Catharines. That same month, Paul proposed to her. She instantly said yes.

Paul's life, however, seemed to be slowly unravelling. He suddenly quit his job at Price Waterhouse, feeling that it didn't offer him enough in the way of advancement. He worked for a Toronto accounting firm for a few months in January 1990 and also tried farming worms, but he preferred smuggling cigarettes across the U.S.–Canada border. He could easily clear several thousand dollars a month packing his Capri with cheap cigarettes, though it was still not enough money to sustain his lifestyle. In March 1990, Paul filed for bankruptcy, citing thousands of dollars in credit card debt. He went on employment insurance and eventually left Toronto, moving in with the Homolkas. The Homolkas had long referred to Paul as their "weekend son" and had no qualms about him living with them, especially with the wedding date scheduled for June 1991. They were enamoured with their future son-in-law.

Then on December 23, 1990, tragedy struck the Homolka family. It was late at night when Karla called for an ambulance, stating that her younger sister Tammy Lyn wasn't breathing. The paramedics who responded to the call found Tammy Lyn in Karla's

room, covered in vomit, with a strange burn mark on
her face. Although the paramedics tried their best,
Tammy Lyn died on the way to the hospital. She was
only 15.

Because of the suspicious nature of Tammy Lyn's
death, police from St. Catharines attended the Homolka
household that night and interviewed the family. Both
Karel and Dorothy had already gone to bed and had
only known something was wrong when the ambulance pulled up. Karla and Paul told the police that
the trio had stayed up to watch a movie. Everyone
had been drinking that night, including Tammy Lyn.
She had just vomited and stopped breathing, they told
the police. Paul was visibly distraught, crying and
shouting, pounding his head against the wall. The
police had to stop Karla from loading several vomit-
soaked blankets into the washing machine.

According to the medical examiner, Tammy Lyn
had died from choking on her own vomit. When
asked, Paul postulated that the burn on her face might
have occurred when he and Karla had dragged Tammy
Lyn from the recreation room into Karla's bedroom.
No one bothered asking them why they had moved
her body in the first place.

Tammy Lyn Homolka was buried on December 27,
1990, four days shy of her 16th birthday. The Homolkas packed her coffin with trinkets and mementos,
including a photo of Paul and Karla, as well as a ring
Paul often wore. When friends later asked the family

how they had survived the ordeal, Dorothy credited Paul with being the strong one in the group.

That strength, however, didn't seem to count for much in the Homolka household. Because by mid-January, Dorothy made it clear to Karla that she and Karel wanted Paul out of their house. Their grief was private, Dorothy tried to explain, and they needed some time alone as a family. Karla wouldn't hear of it. By the end of the month, she and Paul moved into a pink clapboard home on 57 Bayview Drive in Port Dalhousie, St. Catharines. The rent was exorbitant—over $1000 per month—and Paul still wasn't working. By then Karla knew how Paul was making his money, but she didn't seem to mind. She didn't bat an eyelash when Paul turned one of the guest bedrooms into a recording studio. He was going to be a rapper, he said. The next Vanilla Ice.

Despite the Homolkas' efforts to curtail their daughter's spending, both Paul and Karla were determined to host the wedding of the century. They were married on June 29, 1991, at St. Mark's Anglican Church at Niagara-on-the-Lake. The celebration was complete with a carriage ride, champagne and stuffed pheasant. Paul made sure to invite as many people as possible and made no secret of his preference for money over material gifts.

The couple was the spitting image of Ken and Barbie, a young attractive couple with what friends and family thought was an unlimited future filled with success and love.

Not far away, that same day, police officers were pulling the first concrete blocks of Leslie Mahaffy's remains from Lake Gibson.

The investigation into Leslie Mahaffy's murder was going nowhere fast.

There were no witnesses and even less forensic clues. About the only lead the police had to go on was the cement in which her remains had been encased. Police quickly identified the cement as Kwik Mix, a cement mix commonly sold at Beaver Lumber. Although they tried to track down people in the area who had purchased the cement, they could only interview those who had paid with a credit card. They had no way of finding anyone who had paid cash.

The police also clued in on the black paint that coated one of the concrete caskets containing Mahaffy's remains, identifying it as an industrial paint often used on engines and motors. That led them to investigate Jonathan Yeo, an ex-con with a history of sexual aggression who worked at a steel mill and had access to a similar type of paint. But the investigation fell through on August 20 when Yeo killed himself after kidnapping and killing a Burlington teenager named Nina de Villiers.

Inspector Vince Bevan, who headed the Mahaffy investigation, was also interested in John Peter Stark, a neighbour of Yeo's who was a suspect in the disappearance of Julie Stanton, his teenage daughter's best friend. Stanton's body, however, had never been recovered, and the police had no direct evidence implicating him in Mahaffy's disappearance.

Bevan contracted a psychologist and psychiatrist working out of Pentanguishene to develop a criminal profile of the killer. They concluded that the man was most likely bright and organized and would appear normal to the outside world. He was likely a white-collar worker with a new house, who lived alone and might be using child pornography. The man had probably taken Leslie on a spur-of-the-moment decision, not deliberately planning to take her. If he wasn't caught, he would likely kill again.

In April 1992, officers from the Mahaffy investigation met with members of the Federal Bureau of Investigation (FBI) in Buffalo, New York. Since the FBI had developed criminal profiling as an investigative tool, Bevan reasoned they might be able to help. The FBI deduced that the crimes were sexually motivated, and the great effort the killer had gone to in hiding Mahaffy's body spoke to the fact that he had fantasized about it for a long time. He had disposed of her body in Lake Gibson because he was familiar with the area. He was most likely a labourer, someone who worked with his hands. Whoever the killer was, he was now under a great deal of stress, and his behaviour was likely to change. He might start abusing drugs and alcohol or become very religious.

Bevan, however, had no suspects that fit either profile. The Mahaffy investigation was at a standstill, and there was little he could do about it.

At 6:00 PM on April 16, the Niagara Regional Police received a frantic call from Doug and Donna French, residents of St. Catharines. Their 15-year-old daughter, Kristen, had not returned home from school, and none of her friends or her boyfriend knew where she was.

The police responded quickly to the call because Kristen was not the kind of girl to run away or disappear for no reason. She left Holy Cross High School every day just before 3:00 PM and always returned home immediately to feed her dog and let him out of his pen. She was an honours student, an alternate on the school rowing team and an accomplished figure skater. She had a boyfriend, Elton, with whom she had been involved since August of the previous year.

The police spent most of the night and the following morning interviewing Kristen's friends, family and classmates. Staff searched every corner of the school while police dug through her locker. Kristen's parents and friends took to the streets in a massive search that yielded nothing.

At 10:20 AM on April 17, the police responded to a call at Grace Lutheran Church, which was on Kristen's route home from school. One of the parishioners had found a brown loafer in the middle of the parking lot. The shoe contained a special orthopedic lift Kristen had to use because her right leg was shorter than her left. Police spent the next day picking over the church lot, tagging cigarette butts and vacuuming the lawn for trace evidence. In the end, they ended up with a ripped fragment of a map of Scarborough and a lock of brown hair, which was later determined to have been cut off of Kristen's head.

By Saturday afternoon the police had a lead that Bevan believed was the best so far. A woman travelling in the area told police that she had seen a brief struggle in the parking lot. It had taken place near a vehicle, a cream-coloured car that resembled a Camaro or a Trans Am. After taking the witness through several books of cars, Bevan concluded the woman had seen a 1982 Chevrolet Camaro.

The task of finding the actual Camaro involved in the incident, however, was daunting. At the time of French's abduction, there were approximately 37,000 late 1970s or early 1980s Camaros registered in Ontario, with 4000 in the Niagara region alone. Police officers pulled over every cream-coloured Camaro they saw, sometimes even pulling over the same Camaro more than once in the course of a single day. Large roadside billboards were erected with a picture of a 1981 Camaro, "which was stylistically different from the 1982 model," and a phone number, asking people who had seen the car to call. Eventually, the police invited Camaro owners to have their cars checked voluntarily at detachments. After the inspection, officers affixed a sticker to the car so that other police officers would know the car had already been inspected.

The Camaro wasn't Bevan's only angle, though. Four days after French's disappearance, he called a New Jersey psychic for her input, and she promptly

requested that Bevan mail her a photo of Kristen and
a memento. He chose a hair barrette. Bevan also had
one witness hypnotized to recall the exact colour of
the vehicle. Two weeks after French disappeared,
Niagara officers went to the FBI headquarters in
Quantico, Virginia, to consult again with the profiling
unit. The FBI suggested that the Mahaffy and French
murders were not connected and that French had
been the victim of two male assailants. One was dom-
inant, the other submissive. They had low self-esteem
and were considered to be inseparable.

On April 30, the same day that investigators arrived
in the U.S., Kristen French's body was found. A man
looking for scrap metal had stumbled upon a nude
corpse in a ditch along a rural road known as Sideroad
One, near an orchard. Bevan knew instantly it was
French because the body was missing the tip of its left
pinky finger, the same as Kristen. Her hair had been
sheared off, her face severely bruised and battered.
The medical examiner was not able to establish a time
of death—she could have been dead 24 hours or two
weeks. Forensic investigators scoured the scene,
removing hairs and fibres from the body and photo-
graphing it extensively.

Kristen's body, police noted, had been dumped only
a few hundred metres from Leslie Mahaffy's grave.

Faced with the deaths of two teenage girls and
mounting criticism of the investigation, the province
had to act publicly to quell the fears of Ontarians. On
May 5, Inspector Vince Bevan was formally appointed

head of the Green Ribbon Task Force investigating the deaths of Leslie Mahaffy and Kristen French.

Within one week, the task force knocked on the front door of 57 Bayview Drive. An Ontario police officer having breakfast at Smitty's had struck up a conversation by chance with one of Bernardo's friends, Van Smirnis. Smirnis told the officer that Bernardo was a violent deviant with a penchant for aggression. Bernardo had told Smirnis that he had once raped a woman, and as far as Smirnis knew, he also beat Karla. Almost two weeks after receiving the tip, officers from the Green Ribbon Task Force descended on the Bernardo home to interview Paul.

The interview lasted less than half an hour. Bernardo voluntarily admitted he had once been questioned in connection with the Scarborough rapes because of his likeness to the composite sketch. He told the officers that, on April 16, the day French had disappeared, he was home alone, working on his rap album. He had never owned a Camaro. The only car he currently owned was the sporty Nissan 240 SX sitting out in the driveway.

Desperate for leads, Bevan decided it was time to re-examine Leslie Mahaffy. He arranged for an order to exhume her remains, and upon re-examining the torso that day, examiners found two areas of bruising on Mahaffy's back, both asymmetrical, on each side of her spine. It was the only new discovery made during the second autopsy. Leslie's remains were re-interred later that night.

Despite any real evidence to the contrary, Bevan was convinced that because French's remains were found so close to Mahaffy's, the two cases must be linked. He was ready to turn to the public for their help, but he did so in an unusual way. On July 21, 1992, a 90-minute re-enactment entitled "The Abduction of Kristen French" aired on TV in Ontario. In the re-creation, the police for the first time linked Mahaffy and French's deaths. The move generated thousands of tips, none of which helped. The re-enactment also served to outrage the media, who were never told that the two killings might be connected.

As the summer of 1992 drew to a close, Leslie Mahaffy and Kristen French's killer was no closer to being caught.

The emergency room doctor who treated Karla Homolka on January 6, 1993, later described her condition as one of the worst cases of domestic abuse he had ever seen.

Homolka had been brought to hospital by her family that night, after receiving tips from Karla's coworkers that she was coming to work with visible bruises. Police investigators who responded to the complaint found a woman with large, deep bruises under her eyes as well as on other areas of her body. She told the police that Paul had beaten her with a flashlight the night before. Homolka was hospitalized for three days, during which time the police arrested Bernardo and charged him with one count of assault with a weapon.

Karla never returned to 57 Bayview Drive. Upon discharge from hospital, Karla moved into an apartment
with her aunt and uncle.

On February 1, 1993, Kim Johnston, the scientist
given the task of testing all of the DNA samples of the
Scarborough suspects, called Steve Irwin from the Centre for Forensic Sciences with news that turned the
entire Scarborough Rapist investigation on its head.
She had found a DNA match between a suspect and
samples taken from three of the rapes.

The DNA belonged to Paul Bernardo.

It had taken almost two years for the Centre for
Forensic Sciences to complete the DNA-matching
work. Bernardo's sample was one of five of the 230
total samples that were selected for DNA analysis,
based on both his likeness to the composite sketch and
the fact that he was a non-secretor.

The sexual assault squad acted quickly. They immediately put Bernardo under surveillance and tapped
his phone. They interviewed Dorothy and Karel
Homolka and made arrangements to interview Karla.
But before meeting with Homolka, the Toronto Metropolitan police called a meeting with Bevan from the
Green Ribbon Task Force and informed him that his
group should start looking at Bernardo as a possible
suspect in the Mahaffy and French murders.

One week after receiving the news on the DNA
match, three detectives met with Karla and interviewed

her for five hours. Although they told her they were investigating Paul for the rapes in Scarborough, they also asked her other questions about the murders of French and Mahaffy. They asked Karla about a Mickey Mouse watch she was wearing, one that closely resembled a watch French had worn. They also took Karla's fingerprints to compare to a set pulled off the torn section of the map of Scarborough that was found at the church parking lot where French had been taken from. When the detectives left, they had little more information than when they had arrived. Karla told them all about the abuse she had suffered at Paul's hands but little else.

On February 12, 1993, Crown prosecutor Murray Segal received a phone call from Ray Houlahan, one of Segal's regional prosecutors. Houlahan had received a phone call that day from George Walker, who was a well-respected criminal lawyer in Ontario. Walker told Houlahan that he was representing Karla Homolka and that Homolka was ready to tell the police all about what her husband had done to Leslie Mahaffy and Kristen French.

During their phone conversation, Walker informed Houlahan that Paul Bernardo had kidnapped, sexually assaulted and killed the two teens and that Homolka had been forced to participate. Furthermore, said Walker, there were videotapes detailing much of the allegations. If the Crown offered Karla Homolka immunity from prosecution, she was ready to testify against Bernardo.

Segal, however, was hesitant to concede too quickly. If Karla Homolka knew of the kidnappings and killings and had participated in them, regardless of being beaten by her husband, she could also be convicted of first-degree murder along with Bernardo. Immunity, Segal later told Walker, was not an option. But a lesser sentence might be possible.

Now fuelled by Karla's pending admission, the task force decided it was time to act. On February 17, the arrest team descended on the pink clapboard home at 57 Bayview Drive, arrested Paul Bernardo and took him to the Halton Region police headquarters in Oakville for interrogation. After Bernardo was processed and fingerprinted, officers from both Toronto and the Green Ribbon Task Force took turns interviewing him over the course of eight hours. Bernardo, however, wasn't giving anything up beyond idle chit chat and his promise as a white rapper. He was lodged in custody overnight and taken before a judge the following morning.

Much to the titillation of the media, Paul Bernardo wasn't the only Bernardo on the court docket that morning. On that same day in that same courthouse, Ken Bernardo, Paul's own father, was being sentenced on charges of sexually assaulting his daughter, Paul's sister.

Two days later, investigators again descended on the Bernardo home, tearing it apart for trace evidence and forensic clues. They pulled up floors, tore out walls and took apart plumbing. They seized books and clothes. They found a list describing, in chronological order, the rapes committed in Scarborough.

They also found a videotape containing sexually explicit images of two separate women with Karla and Paul, but neither woman could be identified. One of the women looked as though she might be unconscious, but no one could tell for sure.

The police had Karla's confession, but just how involved she was in the murders would remain to be seen.

Fresh off a seven-week stay at a psychiatric hospital during which time she was kept heavily sedated and was diagnosed with post-traumatic stress disorder and depression, Karla Homolka signed off on her plea resolution with the Crown.

Under the terms of the deal, Homolka would testify against Paul Bernardo at his trial. In exchange, she would plead guilty to two counts of manslaughter. The Crown would recommend she serve her sentence at a psychiatric facility and also make a recommendation for early parole after serving the minimum required time of four years and four months. In total, Homolka would serve two concurrent 10-year sentences for the killings of Leslie Mahaffy and Kristen French. Furthermore, though no additional charge would be laid, she would serve an additional two years concurrently on each charge for her participation in what was revealed to be the drugging, rape and inadvertent killing of her own sister, Tammy Lyn Homolka.

On May 14, 1993, Karla sat down with detectives at a motel in Whitby, Ontario, and began her confession. According to Karla, Paul had been upset that Karla was not a virgin when they met. Consequently, in Paul's mind, to make up for this, Karla had to find a virgin for him. Paul quickly turned his attention to Tammy Lyn as a suitable sacrifice. Determined to keep her man happy, Karla scoured the pharmacology books at the vet clinic, looking for a way to knock Tammy out so that Paul could have his way with her. Karla eventually settled on combination of Halcion, a sleeping pill, and halothane, an anaesthetic often used at the vet clinic to put animals under before surgery.

On the night of December 23, 1990, Paul plied Tammy Lyn with alcoholic drinks laced with the crushed Halcion that Karla had obtained by prescription. Once the rest of the Homolka family had gone to bed and Tammy Lyn had passed out, Paul and Karla quickly began their assault. While Karla held a rag soaked in halothane over her sister's mouth, Paul proceeded to rape her, capturing the entire assault on videotape.

Suddenly, Tammy Lyn stopped breathing, and she vomited. The pair quickly dragged her into Karla's bedroom, dressed her and called 911. They hid the pills and the halothane, as well as the camcorder, before the police arrived.

Although seemingly traumatized by the event, Paul still insisted on finding a sex slave, someone who could satisfy both his and Karla's desires on command. It was Paul, Karla told the detectives, who decided to kidnap Leslie Mahaffy on June 15, 1991. He had been out stealing licence plates to use during his cross-border smuggling runs, when he ran into Leslie behind her house. He brought her home, said Karla, though she didn't actually see Leslie until the following morning. When she awoke, Karla told the police, she was irritated to find that Paul had let Leslie drink champagne from their good champagne glasses. Karla said that Paul made her do things with Leslie she would never normally do. They took turns with the camera, with Paul either raping Leslie or telling Karla what he wanted the two of them to do.

Paul later stated to Karla that they had to kill Leslie because she had seen their faces. Homolka told the police she gave Leslie two sleeping pills and let her cuddle her oversized stuffed animal, "Bunky," before Paul came up from the basement with a black electrical cord and strangled her.

They kept Mahaffy's body in their storage room that weekend because Dorothy and Karel were coming over to celebrate Father's Day. That night, after her parents left, Karla said that Bernardo took out his power saw and used it to hack Leslie's body into pieces. He purchased, with cash, several bags of cement at a nearby Beaver Lumber store and used the cement to entomb Leslie's remains. Then they drove to Lake Gibson and dropped the cement chunks into the water off a small bridge on Faywell road.

Kristen's abduction, said Karla, had been more deliberate. Karla and Paul had spent most of April 16 looking for a new girl when they spotted French walking home from school. While Paul stayed in the passenger's seat, Karla got out of the car, holding a map of Scarborough in her hand, and waved French over on the pretence of asking for directions. When she approached, Paul sprang out of the car, shoved a knife in Kristen's face and pushed her into the back seat. What followed over the next several days was almost a repeat of their brutalization of Leslie Mahaffy. Again, Bernardo made Karla participate. Again, Paul videotaped much of the rape. Again, he decided French had to die because she had seen their faces, and he choked her to death.

Leslie had been frightened, said Karla. French had been more compliant, hoping they would eventually let her go.

The police went over Karla's story with her again and again over the course of several days. They checked their facts with her and showed her still photos pulled from the one sex tape they had found so far. Homolka told them she wasn't sure who the women in the video were, but that they could be either Tammy, Leslie or Kristen.

Four days later, Paul Bernardo was officially charged by police with two counts each of first-degree murder, kidnapping, forcible confinement and aggravated sexual assault and one count of performing an indignity to a human body.

Shortly afterwards, Karla made her first appearance in court. She was released on $110,000 bail until her trial, on the condition that she live at home and never leave her parents' house without at least one of them with her, and she was not to use drugs or alcohol. She was also required to check in with Bevan by phone every day.

On June 28, Karla's "trial" began. Although Karla pleaded guilty to two counts of manslaughter, the Crown was still required to prove the essential elements of the crime.

The first few days of Karla's trial were consumed by arguments about media coverage. Whereas the Crown wanted Justice Francis Kovacs to impose a publication ban on the trial, both Bernardo's attorney Ken Murray and several media outlets were determined to fight it. The Crown felt not having the ban would handicap the potential of finding an untainted jury pool for Bernardo's trial. The media argued for the public's right to know, and Murray hired lawyer Tim Breen to argue, somewhat counter-intuitively, that granting a publication ban would violate Bernardo's chance for a fair trial.

After hearing four days of arguments and then adjourning for the Canada Day long weekend, Kovacs split the decision down the middle. Canadian journalists were allowed to stay but were not allowed to publish any details except for Homolka's sentence. Because they were not bound by any Canadian law,

American journalists were barred from the courtroom altogether. So too was the general public.

In less than a day, Karla Homolka was found guilty of manslaughter in the deaths of Leslie Mahaffy and Kristen French. She was sentenced to two concurrent 12-year sentences and was promptly escorted to the Kingston Prison for Women.

The publication ban didn't stop the American media from reporting on the trial anyway. "A Current Affair," an American tabloid TV current events program, detailed Karla's trial and also featured an interview with a gay pimp who claimed to have given Bernardo oral sex in prison. Articles about the trial appeared in the *Sunday Mirror* in Great Britain and the *Washington Post*. Customs officials searched for copies of the *Post* in the cars of Canadians returning to Canada from the U.S. Details also appeared on the Internet, which was accessible to any person with a modem. There was nothing that any of the officials could do about it.

The media coverage, however, was the least of Ken Murray's problems. He was struggling with a difficult ethical situation that would eventually draw the wrath of the entire country.

On July 20, 1993, Tammy Lyn's body was exhumed and re-examined in the hopes of finding traces of Halcion and halothane, as well as any semen stains or pubic hairs. When the body was returned to its coffin, the picture of Paul and Karla was removed before the casket was buried, as was Paul's ring.

Ken Murray was in a heap of trouble. Acting on a tip from his client, Paul Bernardo, Murray had stopped by the Bayview house and searched behind a pot light in the bathroom. He found a bundle of six videotapes, which he later copied and watched. Their contents made him sick to his stomach.

Viewing the videotapes also put the legal aid lawyer in a difficult position. Court precedence, mostly out of the U.S., dictated that he was obligated to hand over to the authorities any physical evidence of a crime. Simply by watching the tapes, he had made himself a material witness in the case and could be called to the stand to testify against his client.

To complicate things further, Murray was also bound by the sacrosanct relationship between attorney and client. Technically, Murray could not divulge any communications between himself and Bernardo. It was a Catch-22, an ethically vicious circle with no easy answer.

On August 15, Murray pleaded with John Rosen, a well-known and respected Toronto defence lawyer, to take over the case. Grudgingly, Rosen accepted.

At a hearing held later, with Murray, Rosen, Austin Cooper (who now represented Ken Murray) and Ray Houlahan, the bundle of six videotapes were handed over to the police.

All six tapes detailed in first-person perspective the horrific, degrading acts Paul Bernardo had perpetrated on Tammy Lyn, Leslie and Kristen. The videotaped assaults weakened the steel of even the most experienced detective. One fact in particular stood out for everyone who watched the tapes: Karla Homolka appeared to be a willing accomplice in each and every one of the rapes.

At one point in the videotape of her sister's assaults, Karla had seemed somewhat reluctant when Paul told her to start digitally penetrating her sister. Her revulsion, though, seemed centred on the fact that Tammy Lyn was having her period, not that she was actively participating in the rape of her sister. Investigators watched with queasy stomachs as Karla licked her unconscious sister's breasts while Paul vaginally and anally raped her.

The videotapes detailing Leslie's imprisonment were even more brutal. Bernardo was merciless in his rape, forcing Leslie to perform oral sex on him and then raping her vaginally and anally over and over again, sometimes at knife point. Paul and Karla traded the camera back and forth repeatedly—Paul videotaping while Leslie performed sex acts on Karla, and Karla videotaping Paul. The rapes were interspersed with footage of Mahaffy either going to the bathroom or washing herself in the shower. From time to time she cried, begging her captors to let her go so she could see her family again. In almost all of the footage, she was blindfolded with an old T-shirt.

As violent as Leslie's rape had been, the tapes detailing Kristen's torture were horrific by comparison, made more so by Kristen's compliance and blatant fear. There was no blindfold this time. Again, Karla and Paul took turns with the camera and with their victim. Paul savaged Kristen at every opportunity, forcing her to perform oral sex and talk to the camera while she did so. She told him she loved him and that all the girls at her school should want to have sex with him because he was "the king."

Again, he raped her vaginally and anally. Again, he videotaped her going to the bathroom, then showering, even giving her specific instructions on how to clean herself. He had Karla dress up in a schoolgirl's outfit similar to Kristen's and filmed the pair playing "The Perfume Game." In the game, Karla and Kristen each tried on different scents, then sniffed one another. "The one who smells the best," said Paul, "won't get f****d up the ass." Kristen lost the competition.

The indignities continued. In between the rapes and beatings, Paul took Kristen into the bathroom and had her sit in the Jacuzzi tub. He urinated on her, then tried to defecate on her but couldn't. He taunted Kristen with a knife, placing it on the floor in front of her and goading her to grab it and stab him. She never tried.

The last footage of Kristen French alive showed her tied up on the bedroom floor.

"I don't know how your wife can stand you," she said.

Paul told her to shut up. Then the screen went blank.

The police eventually sat down with Homolka and went through each videotape with her, having her recite over and over again exactly what was happening. It was a macabre experience for the officers, listening as Homolka threw around words such as "blowjob" and "fingering" as though they were common verbs.

The entire experience, nevertheless, confirmed what the police had long suspected. Ken Murray had been correct. The Crown had, in fact, made a deal with the devil. From their perspective, Karla Homolka had been a willing participant in each rape, and for that she would serve only 12 years in jail.

The rage that came with this realization was further fuelled by Murray's actions. If Bernardo's former lawyer had handed over the videotapes as soon as he had found them, the deal would never have been necessary, and Karla would have been tried on charges similar to her husband's.

By this point nothing really surprised the officers working the case. When Karla finally came forward and admitted that one of the women in the first videotape found by police had also been raped, they opened another investigation. The woman, only ever known as Jane Doe in the public eye, had worked with Homolka at the pet store. Bernardo and Homolka had invited her over one night, drugged her and raped her. Later, when she was conscious, she refused to have vaginal sex with Bernardo. She had no idea she had been raped.

On another occasion, again after drugging and raping Jane Doe, Karla was forced to call 911 because Jane had stopped breathing. Paul and Karla had again used the cocktail of Halcion and halothane to subdue their victim. Shortly after Karla made the call, however, Jane started breathing again so Karla called 911 back and cancelled the ambulance.

After reviewing the evidence, the Crown decided to grant Karla blanket immunity for her role in the Jane Doe rapes. Paul was charged with sexual assault.

On May 1, 1995, jury selection in the Paul Bernardo trial began. One thousand people were notified of jury duty, and they all congregated at a local hotel ballroom. After three days, all 12 members of the jury, eight men and four women, were selected to serve.

The trial was one of the most sensational in Canadian criminal history. On its opening day, reporters, family members and members of the public started lining up outside the courthouse at 4:00 AM to get a seat.

Both Rosen and Houlahan were in difficult positions. Rosen had to convince 12 people that his client was guilty of a lesser charge of murder because of his wife's complicity, even though most of the evidence against Bernardo was captured on videotape. Houlahan had to defend the Crown's deal with Homolka and also hope that Karla stood up under what was sure to be a withering cross-examination by Rosen. Bernardo's fate was sealed before he even entered the courtroom. The exact length of that fate, however, was still up in the air.

Members of the public watching from the gallery squirmed in their chairs as they listened to a litany of police officers and family members testify one right after the other, making the case for the Crown. The crux of their case, however, lay in both the videotapes and their star witness, Karla Homolka.

Associate Justice Chief Justice Patrick LeSage had already dealt with the issue of the videotapes. Members of the victims' family, along with the defence, had tried to persuade LeSage to prohibit the use of the videotapes in the trial. LeSage decided to compromise: only he, the jury, the accused and the defence and crown attorneys would be allowed to watch the videos of Tammy Lyn, Leslie and Kristen's rapes. The spectators would only be permitted to hear the audio. There were no restrictions placed on any of the other videotapes.

The Crown first chose to play for the entire courtroom a video in which Karla and Paul had sex shortly after Tammy Lyn's death. The shocking part was that Karla was pretending to be Tammy Lyn while she and Paul were having sex.

"I loved it when you f****d my little sister," Karla said at one point.

Even though the gallery did not see the actual rape tapes, they heard everything that had happened, from Paul's beatings to Kristen and Leslie's screams. Many people in the gallery got up and excused themselves from their seats, never returning. At one point, one of the jurors fixed Bernardo with a withering stare.

On June 23, the Crown finally put Karla Homolka on the stand. Over the course of nine days, Houlahan took her through each attack and each rape. He made no secret of Karla's deal with the Crown, introducing it immediately in his questioning. Karla talked about the beatings she suffered at Paul's hands, his endless, perverted sexual demands and his emotional and verbal abuse. When he was unhappy with her, he made her sleep on their bedroom floor.

"Stupidly I loved him. For the most part he was treating me nicely. I kept hoping things would improve."

When the Crown concluded its case, Rosen charged out of his seat, hammering Homolka with questions. He showed her pictures of Tammy Lyn, alive and then lying on a gurney, of Leslie alive and then in pieces on an examination table, of Kristen alive and then dumped in a ditch. He assailed Karla's motives, her character and her psychology, declaring her just as guilty of each assault and death as Bernardo.

More dramatically, he insinuated that Karla and not Paul had been responsible for actually killing Leslie and Kristen. He inferred that the two bruises found on Leslie's torso roughly matched the marks that Karla's knees would have made if she had been kneeling on her, effectively suffocating her. He openly accused Karla of using a rubber mallet to beat Kristen to death when she tried to escape while Paul was away.

Karla responded that she had been blowdrying her hair when Kristen was killed.

Homolka denied all of Rosen's accusations, stepping deftly away from his attempts to draw her in. Over eight days, Rosen continued to hammer away at her, but Homolka refused to give him anything. His dramatics in court were at times engrossing; other times they seemed ludicrous. He paraded the litany of love notes that Karla had written to Paul over their years together, wondering why a woman who claimed to be so traumatized by her abusive husband would stay with him and continue to shower him with affection.

"I was terrified. I was staying with that marriage because he had stuff over my head. Until you've been in that situation, you'd never understand."

When Homolka left the stand, Paul Bernardo took her place to rebut her testimony. He tried to support Rosen's theory that Karla and not he had killed Mahaffy and French, declaring he had not even been in the house when French died.

"We liked having sex slaves in the house," he told the jury matter-of-factly.

Homolka, he said, had also been an active participant when they dismembered Mahaffy's body. According to Paul, they set up a plastic tent in the basement, and Homolka washed each body part as it came free.

Houlahan responded by taking Bernardo through both Mahaffy and French's videotapes, highlighting the screams and the pleas for mercy and release. Bernardo tried to talk his way around the questions, but Houlahan kept rewinding the tapes and playing them again. By the end of his three hours of testimony, Bernardo looked like a beaten man.

The jury agreed. The day after the jury received their instructions from LeSage, Paul Bernardo, 31, was found guilty on all nine counts. Bernardo was automatically sentenced to life in prison, with no chance of parole for 25 years. But that chance was effectively eliminated when the Crown successfully had the courts brand him with "dangerous offender" status, a criminal title for offenders whose release would threaten the public; it effectively keeps them behind bars for life. Bernardo's appeal of his conviction was rejected by the three-judge panel of the Ontario Court of Appeal in less than 30 minutes.

Paul Bernardo is currently incarcerated at the Kingston Penitentiary for Men, serving his life sentence in a four-by-eight cell. Although he will be eligible for parole in 2020, the Crown is unlikely to ever lift his dangerous offender status.

Paul Bernardo's conviction gave way to a new anger in Canada, and the entire brunt of it was aimed squarely at Karla Homolka.

Her own testimony and the videotapes played at her trial revealed to the public just how complicit she

PAUL BERNARDO & KARLA HOMOLKA   123

was in all three deaths. Three hundred thousand people eventually signed a petition protesting the Crown's deal with the devil. One Canadian started up a website on which users could predict the exact day, hour and minute of Homolka's death. No one, the website warns, is allowed to actually cause her death because "murder is wrong."

Homolka, in the meantime, refused to simply fade from the public eye. She served time in Kingston, Joliette, and Sainte-Anne-des-Plaines. At the Joliette institute, in which she lived in one of 10 bungalows with several other inmates, Karla again became the focus of public scorn when pictures of her wearing a slinky black dress at a party were released to the media. She was rumoured to have taken a lesbian lover in prison and then was romantically linked with convicted killer Jean-Paul Gerbet. In January 2003, Stephen Williams, already known for his book *Invisible Darkness: The Strange Case of Paul Bernardo and Karla Homolka*, published *Karla, le pacte avec le diable* (A Pact with the Devil). The police quickly began investigating whether Karla had contributed to the book, which would violate the terms of her plea agreement. Ten weeks after first being directed to investigate the matter by the attorney general of Ontario, the *Ottawa Citizen* reported that the police had not yet read the book.

Although every Canadian convicted of a crime becomes eligible for mandatory release after serving two-thirds of their sentence, Karla became one of the few who did not. She was sent to Saskatoon to be evaluated for release, but the National Parole Board later made the decision to keep her in jail for the full 12 years, stating she was likely to re-offend. When her sentence finally did expire, the Crown successfully petitioned a Québec judge to impose restrictions on her movements. That order was later overturned by another Québec court.

In 2005, Hollywood decided to cash in on the Bernardo–Homolka story. *Karla*, starring Laura Prepon as Homolka and Misha Collins as Bernardo, debuted at the Montréal World Film Festival. The movie, which the victims' family lawyer Tim Danson called "sensational and exploitive," screened at only a handful of Canadian theatres. There are currently no plans to release the movie on DVD in Canada, though copies did go on sale in the U.S. in June 2006.

Karla Homolka's (aka Karla Leanne Teale) current whereabouts are not known, but she is believed to be living in Longueuil, Québec, just off Montréal's south shore. She is not currently bound by any court order.

CHAPTER FOUR

Keith Hunter Jesperson
(1955–)

Nebraska, September 1995

IT WAS ALL THE STATE TROOPER COULD DO NOT TO VOMIT.

He was standing just off the side of Interstate 80, not too far from the tiny town of Gothenburg, Nebraska. The trooper tried not to look at it, but like so many of the motorists he caught rubbernecking at a nasty car accident scene, he could not look away. The information he'd been given was very specific. If he looked in this particular area, he would likely find what investigators in both Nebraska and Wyoming were looking for.

The information was right on the money.

There was no doubt that he was looking at what had once been a female human being, but that was about all he could tell from the putrefied mass of flesh that he was now taping off. Where there were once arms and legs, only bloody stumps remained. There was no face, no skin left on the torso. The months between her death and today had done a number on what little human flesh remained; the body had decayed naturally with the help of the animals in the area.

There was one patch of skin left that looked like it belonged to an ankle. The trooper bent down to get a closer look and came face to face with a tattoo of the classic cartoon character Tweety Bird. The adorable little rascal who had tormented Sylvester in the cartoons of his youth was now, ironically, flipping him the bird.

After taping off the area, the trooper walked back to his parked patrol car on the shoulder of the Interstate. He called in what he found to dispatch, then sat back to await the arrival of the forensics team. His stomach slowly settled, but he could feel a headache coming on.

He closed his eyes against the headache, but every time he did he saw a lump of decaying, putrid flesh that had once been a young woman. Tweety continued to taunt him with his indecent gesture.

What kind of monster, he wondered, could do this to someone?

Investigators in Oregon were definitely looking at an open-and-shut murder case. It was a strange case, of that there could be no doubt, but they already had their suspects in custody.

On January 22, 1990, a cyclist working his way above the Columbia River Gorge 15 kilometres east of Portland came across a shocking discovery. When investigators arrived on scene, the cyclist pointed them to the body that was lying face-up on the embankment.

It was a woman, they could instantly see, and a young one at that, probably no older than 26 or 27. The cause of death also appeared to be fairly obvious—there was a white nylon rope wrapped tightly around her neck.

Her bra and shirt had been pushed up over her breasts, with her panties and jeans pushed down to her ankles. Upon closer investigation, crime scene investigators found that someone had neatly cut out the button-fly of her jeans, leaving an almost-perfect semicircle.

An autopsy confirmed that the woman, who they had problems identifying, had been strangled to death. The police released a description of their Jane Doe to the media, who buried the story deep in the newspaper or at the back end of a televised newscast. Eight days after the body was found, a woman who saw one of the newscasts eventually came down to the sheriff's office. Through choking sobs and flowing tears, she positively identified the Jane Doe as her 23-year-old daughter, Taujna Bennett.

Taujna had left her mother's home shortly after lunch, the day before she had been found, bound for one of her favourite destinations, the B & I Tavern. Taujna, her mother and friends revealed, was a friendly woman with a slight mental challenge. She was trusting and ignorant of the evils in the world. She greeted everyone she met with a huge bear hug.

Investigators interviewed the bar staff and learned that Taujna had spent most of the afternoon and night alternating between beer and coolers, playing pool with two men. At around 5:00 PM, Taujna approached bartender Carol Copeland and asked her if she would go dancing with them after Carol was done work. Carol refused, trying to warn Taujna of the danger of going out with men she had only just met. Taujna had brushed her off with a laugh. The next time Copeland looked up, at approximately 8:00 PM, Taujna was gone.

The police initially focused on the description they received of the two blond men with whom Taujna had been playing pool with for most of the afternoon and evening. Within weeks of her murder, detectives had two suspects in custody. Neither suspect, however, was tall or blond and only one of them was a man.

The woman who had first approached the police claiming information about Taujna Bennett's murder had seemed so unlike a murderer that it took the police several interviews before they really start believing her. Her name was Laverne Pavlinac, and she was a 57-year-old grandmother. The woman had been involved in an abusive relationship for 10 years with a man almost 20 years her junior, John Sosnovske. A teary-eyed Pavlinac sat down with detectives in the first interview and told them she knew that Sosnovske was responsible for Bennett's murder.

Pavlinac's story, however, changed with each successive interview. During a second sit-down with detectives, she told them that John had forced her to help dispose of the body near the Columbia Gorge.

In a third interview, Pavlinac told police that John had forced her to participate in kidnapping Bennett, then in raping her. It had been her job, said Pavlinac, to hold the rope around Taujna's neck while John raped her. By the time Sosnovske had finished, Pavlinac realized that Bennett was no longer breathing.

Pavlinac went even further, producing a neatly excised fly of a pair of jeans she said they had removed from Bennett's body. Pavlinac's statements were enough for police to bring Sosnovske in for questioning. He categorically denied everything yet failed two lie-detector tests. Also, forensic investigators had found a brown hair on Bennett's corpse that closely matched Sosnovske's.

Pavlinac took the case one step further, driving out to the Gorge with detectives and pointing out the general area where they had dumped Bennett's body. She was off by about five metres, but it had been dark when they had allegedly committed the crime, so the police gave her the benefit of the doubt. Investigators took what they had on file to the district attorney, who recommended charges of murder against both Pavlinac and Sosnovske.

Pavlinac at first readily confessed to the crime, while Sosnovske maintained his innocence. Suddenly, Pavlinac had a change of heart, refusing to plead guilty to the murder. She explained to police that it had all been a ruse, that she had only confessed to police to try to get the abusive Sosnovske out of her life. Instead of confessing, Pavlinac went to trial, where she took the stand in her own defence. Her lawyer argued for hours during the closing statements, trying to convince the jury that her client was not responsible for Bennett's murder. The deputy district attorney trying the case, however, played Pavlinac's tape-recorded confession for the jury one last time. It was enough to convince the 12-member panel to find Pavlinac guilty. She was sentenced to life in prison with the possibility of parole after 10 years.

Seeing what happened in Pavlinac's trial, Sosnovske also had a change of heart. Knowing a guilty verdict in a trial could get him the death penalty, he instead pleaded no contest to the charge of killing Taujna Bennett, in order to save his life. He was also sentenced to life in prison

No sooner had the book closed on her case, however, than Pavlinac started recanting her story. John was abusive, she tried to tell the police, and the only way she could get rid of him was to have him arrested. She had guessed about the location of Bennett's body by watching the odometer in the police car and had cut the fly out of her daughter's jeans. She was just trying to get away from John.

No one would listen. All the evidence accumulated to that date pointed to her and John's guilt. The police and the county closed the file on Taujna Bennett's murder, deeming it solved. Pavlinac and Sosnovske were left to rot in the Oregon State Penitentiary for their crimes.

Starting in 1992, the bodies of dead women began showing up all over the United States.

On August 30, 1992, police responded to a report of a dead body found 15 kilometres north of Blythe, California, covered in tumbleweeds. The female remains were already significantly decayed, a sign that the body had been lying in the foothills near the Arizona border for several weeks. The arms of the woman were bound with duct tape. An autopsy revealed she had been strangled to death. Despite their best efforts, the police were unable to find out who she was. She was labelled a Jane Doe, her death filed as suspicious and eventually forgotten.

One month later, the body of Cynthia Lynn Rose, 32, was found along U.S. Highway 99 outside Turlock, California. Her body was also significantly decayed, but police found no evidence of foul play at the scene. Her death was ruled as a drug overdose, and her body was released for burial.

In November 1992, detectives responded to a report of a dead body found in Salem, Oregon. The body, they eventually determined, belonged to Laurie Ann Pentland, a 26-year-old known prostitute. Her body was found in a deserted area behind a store called G.I. Joe's. An autopsy showed that she had been strangled, but because of the transient nature of her lifestyle, the police had little success in tracking down any leads. The investigation quickly grew cold.

In July 1993, the police found the body of a woman on the side of a state highway, west of Santa Nella,

California. The body was still relatively intact; it appeared she had only been dead for a couple of days. There were no obvious signs of foul play, however. Similar to Cynthia Lynn Rose before her, the death of this Jane Doe was ruled a drug overdose, and she was promptly forgotten.

One year later, the investigation into her death was reopened.

The letters all arrived within months of one another. They were sadistic, arrogant and strangely proud. Each one confessed that the writer of the letter was responsible for the death of Taujna Bennett, even though Bennett's murderers were already in jail. And each note was also signed with a crudely drawn happy face.

The first letter arrived at the courthouse in Clark County, Washington. The writer admitted straightforwardly that he, and not Pavlinac and Sosnovske, was responsible for the death of Taujna Bennett. The writer gave details of taking Bennett's Walkman and two dollars from her purse, as well as cutting the fly from her jeans after he had killed her.

Nothing came of the letter.

In 1994, within weeks of one another, two more letters appeared in the mailboxes of *The Oregonian* newspaper. The first letter again claimed responsibility for Bennett's murder, except it referred to her as "Sonya" and not Taujna. The second letter referred to the recent murder of a "street person" in Corning,

California. Corning was not too far from Santa Nella, where the Jane Doe's body was found. Upon receipt of the second letter, detectives in California again began investigating the Jane Doe's death. Besides the letters affixed with their trademark happy face, the detectives had little else to go on.

"I do not want to kill again and I want to protect my family from grief," the letter read. "I would tear it apart."

In September 1994, a road construction crew working along Interstate 10 west of Crestview, Florida, came across the petrified remains of a human body on the side of the highway. Forensic investigators recovered the bones from the side of the road but could do little with them. From the size and shape of the pelvis, and by analyzing the age of the bones, they determined the body to be that of a woman who had likely been 40 years old at the time of her death. Forensic anthropologists attempted to reconstruct a likeness for her face but had little success in attracting any leads as a result of their work.

Over a year later on March 10, 1995, thousands of kilometres from Florida, in Washougal, Washington, police found the remains of another woman. Unlike the other cases that had popped up across the western half of the country over the last few years, this case had leads. The remains were identified as those of Julie Ann Winningham, 41, of Camas, Washington. She had been strangled and her body dumped over the side of an embankment on Highway 14.

After identifying the body, Detective Rick Buckner of the Clark County Sheriff's Department began to paint a picture of Winningham's life. Although a known drug addict and party girl with a noteworthy criminal record, she had still been someone's daughter and friend. After interviewing members of her family, Buckner learned that Winningham had recently spent a lot of time with a long-haul truck driver whom Winningham had actually taken to calling her fiancée. His name was Keith Hunter Jesperson.

A quick check revealed the name of Jesperson's trucking company and that he didn't have a criminal record. The only public record on file was a divorce ruling in Yakima County five years previously. According to the file, Jesperson had three children from the marriage. The wife, a woman named Rose, had since remarried. Jesperson, Buckner learned, was actually Canadian by birth.

Jesperson's trucking company provided Buckner with a copy of his itinerary, showing that he would be travelling through Pennsylvania, Texas, New Mexico and Arizona on his current haul. He was scheduled to pick up a load in Las Cruces, New Mexico, on March 22. Buckner made the trip to New Mexico, drafting another detective from Clark County and several Las Cruces deputies into helping him. When Jesperson drove up to the Las Cruces fairgrounds, Buckner and his partner took no

chances. They arrested the 6'6", 240-pound behe-
moth at gunpoint, handcuffed him and informed him
he was being detained for questioning in the investigation of the death of Julie Ann Winningham.

Jesperson, however, was not cooperative when they
got him back to the Las Cruces office. Despite six hours
of questioning, the giant truck driver refused to answer
the detectives' questions. It had been their only shot.
Despite a strong gut feeling typical of successful investigators, Buckner had no evidence on which to hold
Jesperson. After Jesperson consented to provide blood
and hair samples, as well as photographs and fingerprints, he was returned to his truck and let go.

Two days later, Buckner had no sooner arrived back
at his office in Clark County when the phone rang. It
was Jesperson calling from a restaurant in Arizona.
Buckner watched his tape recorder to make sure it
was working as he listened to Jesperson confess to
Julie Winningham's murder.

At the end of the call, Buckner warned Jesperson to
stay put, then called the nearby sheriff's office to send
some deputies to the restaurant to apprehend him. In
the ensuing days between his confession and extradi-
tion to Washington from Arizona, Buckner and his
team began asking around, trying to find out as much
as they could about their newly confessed killer.

What they found was a human bomb that had
exploded long ago.

Keith Hunter Jesperson was born April 6, 1955, in the community of Chilliwack, BC. He was one of five children born to Leslie Samuel Jesperson and Gladys Bellamy Jesperson. Les was a town alderman who was also known for several small inventions that streamlined harvesting in the hops-growing industry.

Les was also, by Keith's admission, a drunk who believed in corporal punishment and seemed to single out Keith for most of his scorn. Keith was an obedient but easily distracted young boy who preferred his own company to that of other people. He liked fishing for salmon in the nearby rivers or hunting small pests such as gophers and muskrats. More often than not, his father praised him for killing the small creatures.

That praise continued the year when Keith picked up a stray kitten and smashed it into the ground, killing it with his bare hands right in front of his father.

The animal cruelty went on, and then, at Easter 1967, Les moved the entire family south of the border to live in Selah, Washington. Keith's torturous treatment of animals grew to include stray dogs after his father shot and killed Keith's aging Labrador retriever, "Duke." According to Keith, dogs would eventually "piss themselves" whenever he was around.

The young teen also started lighting fires in the far corners of his family's land, watching the flames dance before his eyes. His relationship with his father continued to be difficult, characterized by a random pattern of pulling close and pushing apart. According to Keith, his father singled him out for punishment and ridicule more often than his siblings, yet he spent more time hunting and fishing with Keith than with the others. Gladys' role in the family was to simply hold the family together, which she tried her best to do.

Keith was a little slow growing up, his grades never pushing higher than a C average and more often dropping lower than that. By the time he reached junior high school, he was six-feet tall, which set him up for scorn and ridicule by his classmates. Jesperson, nevertheless, knew what he wanted to do with his life. While the rest of his siblings eventually went off to college or university, Jesperson made it known that he was intent on returning to Canada to become a member of the Royal Canadian Mounted Police.

That dream, however, was dashed in high school when Keith fell while climbing a rope during gym class. The ensuing rough landing on the floor resulted in a severe ankle sprain, which was never treated properly and took years to heal.

After graduating high school, where he had earned a school letter as a wrestler, Keith moved out of the family home and worked full time at a gas station. In 1974, he began dating a waitress named Rose Pernick, and they married on August 2, 1975. He then went to work with his father, who had purchased a wide swath of land in Yakima, Washington, on which he hoped to build a mobile home park called Silver Spur. Keith helped his dad develop the site, where he learned all about plumbing, construction and heavy machinery. It was also Keith's job to kill any stray cats or dogs that wandered onto the property, a duty he performed with gusto. It was a habit that continued even after his three children were born. On more than one occasion, he killed a cat right in front of his daughters or son.

The mobile home park, however, was not the sure moneymaker Les Jesperson had banked on, and the pair was eventually forced to sell their stake. Keith spent the money frivolously on cars, motorcycles and bad loans to friends, realizing too late that he had dug himself and his growing family into a financial hole. He took a series of odd jobs around Yakima before finally landing a job as a truck driver. When he was busiest with work, he was only home for five or six days a month, which began to put a strain his marriage. That stress increased in 1980 when Keith took a job in Elkford, BC, working at a mine. Soon after he moved his family back to Canada, he was caught by a mine security guard trying to leave the site with a pair of company coveralls. Although the Fording Coal Company offered to wipe his slate clean after a year of perfect behaviour if he admitted to the theft, Keith refused and was subsequently fired. He got a job in Lethbridge, Alberta, making truck runs to Calgary but eventually returned to the U.S. in 1984 when his mother was diagnosed with cancer. She died in April 1985. Les mourned by remarrying less than a year later.

After finding work as a trucker, Keith spent more time away from home, and he also started cheating on Rose with the assortment of "lot lizards," who prowled semi-trailer truck stops across the United States. It was the beginning of the end of his marriage. In 1988 he met a woman who he only ever identified as "Peggy," and he saw her whenever he could, mostly because she was an animal in bed. Keith announced to Rose that he wanted a divorce. She and the children moved out days later when he was out on a trucking run.

Keith and Peggy eventually became driving partners, which turned out to be a bad decision. According to Keith, Peggy was not as proficient at driving as he was, and before long, the pair was fighting constantly. They repeatedly broke up and got back together. When they were back together, others told Keith about the other men Peggy was sleeping with behind his back. By January 1990, their partnership was again on the rocks. Peggy left him to go back to an old boyfriend in Knoxville. On the night of January 21, 1990, an angry and bored Keith Jesperson decided to go to the B & I Tavern in Portland for a drink and a few games of pool.

Keith Jesperson tried to kill himself twice on the evening of March 22, 1995, by taking sleeping pills. But each time he woke up, he was more frustrated than before.

Just prior to attempting suicide, Jesperson wrote a letter to Brad, one of his brothers, in which he claimed that he was responsible for more than just one murder.

"I am sorry that I turned out this way. I have been a killer for five years. And have killed eight people. I've assaulted more. I guess I haven't learned anything."

Shortly after his confession and subsequent arrest, Jesperson called Brad and tried to convince him to destroy the letter. He was too late. Brad had already turned the letter over to the police.

Armed with Jesperson's statement in the letter about committing eight murders, Detective Buckner circulated a memo to sheriffs' offices across the U.S. asking for information about unsolved homicides. They received quick response. Police in Oregon were looking for a woman who had disappeared in August 1994, her body found only in March. Investigators in Nevada and Utah also looked into several unsolved murders but found no evidence linking Jesperson to any of them.

Now in jail, Jesperson committed a common sin of most killers: he started bragging. A fellow inmate informed the prison authorities that Jesperson was claiming responsibility for killing a girl named Angela Subrize in either Nebraska or Wyoming. Investigators followed up on the tip, finding that Subrize had called her father, who lived in Colorado, in January 1995 and had charged the call to a credit card belonging to Jesperson's brother. When investigators showed Jesperson a picture of Subrize, he admitted that he had killed her.

The two had met at a hotel bar in Spokane and spent the night together. Jesperson offered to drive her to her father's home in Colorado, but Subrize apparently decided she wanted to go to Indiana instead, to hook up with an old boyfriend. Jesperson told investigators he killed her because she was so anxious to get to Indiana that she wouldn't let him sleep. After he choked her to death, he tied her body underneath the rig of his truck and dragged the corpse for 20 kilometres until there was little left to identify her. He pulled over in Nebraska and dumped her remains at the side of Inter-state 80. A deputy using Jesperson's directions found Subrize's remains days later.

Jesperson, however, had a problem. Officials in Wyoming were convinced he had committed the murder in their state and were eager to get their hands on him. They were not willing to entertain any kind of deal. If they successfully tried Jesperson, he would be sentenced to death.

Oregon also had the death penalty but had not executed anyone since the 1960s. Jesperson knew he had to find a way to keep himself from being extra-dited to Wyoming.

Prison officials also knew that Jesperson had been telling other inmates that he, and not Laverne Pav-linac and John Sosnovske, had murdered Taunja Bennett in 1990. Jesperson had also successfully smuggled a letter out of jail addressed to *The Columbian,* a Vancouver–Washington newspaper, indicating that he was intent on making sure that both Pavlinac and Sosnovske were freed.

The police had already gotten their hands on his three previous letters and were comparing handwriting sam-ples to determine if Jesperson had, in fact, written them. At first they doubted that Jesperson had actually killed Bennett, but the longer they waited, the more noise Jesperson made. He granted interviews to any reporter who would listen to him, in which he repeatedly declared that he could lead investigators to Bennett's purse, an item that had never been recovered.

The police decided to give Jesperson a chance to prove himself. On a day outing in which the confessed killer was kept closely guarded, Jesperson led them to the exact location where he had dumped Bennett's body, then successfully pointed them towards Bennett's purse. Both Jesperson and Pavlinac were given lie-detector tests. Jesperson was found to be telling the truth when admitting he had killed Bennett, while Pavlinac was found to be telling the truth in claiming she hadn't. Faced with this fresh evidence, the state of Oregon started the necessary proceedings to free Pavlinac and Sosnovske.

According to Jesperson, he had met Bennett at the B & I Tavern on January 21, 1990, where he went to play a few games of pool. She had introduced herself to him by giving him a big hug. Although he eventually went back home, he returned to the tavern later that night and asked Bennett if she'd go out for dinner with him. When she said yes, he showed her that he had no money in his wallet but had some at home. Once he got her in the door, he attacked and raped her. He beat her viciously about the head and choked her until she finally died. He returned to the tavern to establish an alibi and later drove out to the Columbia River Gorge and threw Bennett's corpse over the embankment. He cut out the button-fly from her jeans because he was afraid his fingerprints were on it. He spent the rest of the night at a truck stop drinking coffee.

As if the recent events had somehow forced open his conscience, Jesperson began confessing to every murder he had committed. He went even further, at times telling investigators that he was responsible for a total of 166 murders. The first few murder confessions—of Cynthia Lynn Rose, Laurie Ann Pentland, a woman named Claudia in California, a woman named Susanna in Florida, as well as a "street person" in California—seemed promising, but no one believed his claim of 166 victims. He later recanted the number.

In 1992, he had picked up Claudia at a brake-check area outside San Bernardino, California, tied her up with duct tape and raped her repeatedly. He started his ritual of the "death game" with Claudia, choking her until she passed out then reviving her. He did this several times before strangling her to death with his bare hands. He dumped her body just outside Blythe and covered it in tumbleweeds.

The police in California sat up and took interest on hearing this story. They had such a body but had never released the fact she had been bound with duct tape.

Jesperson told the police he had killed Cynthia Lynn Rose at a truck stop outside Turlock, California, because she had let herself into his truck while he was sleeping. He killed Laurie Ann Pentland after he paid her for her services at a truck stop in Wilsonville—she had tried to raise the price on him. He bought the "street person" dinner in Corning, California, and raped her after offering to drive her to Sacramento. All of the victims were choked to death, all but one—Cynthia—were raped, and all but Cynthia were unwilling participants in his death game.

Jesperson was also making a name for himself in prison. Already dubbed "the Happy Face Killer" because of the small drawings he'd included in his letters, Jesperson convinced a friend to start up a website offering a Serial Killer Start-Up Kit. He vacillated between referring to his victims as unfortunate instruments of his rage and "piles of garbage." He continued to toy with the state of Wyoming, claiming he would change his testimony about where he killed Subrize and draw the trial out for as long as possible unless they took the death penalty off the table. He told investigators looking into the Green River murders in Washington a fantastic lie about accidentally running over a woman in Seattle in the 1980s and deciding to bury her remains in an open field. At the same time as he was burying the corpse, another man had appeared and started burying another corpse. The two men went out for coffee afterwards, at which time Jesperson said they discovered they had each killed one of a set of twin sisters.

The Green River investigators openly discredited Jesperson's story, since none of the Green River Killer's murder victims had been sisters, let alone twins.

In October 1995, just before his trial for the murder of Julie Winningham was scheduled to begin, Jesperson entered a guilty plea. The judge in the proceedings sentenced him to life in prison with no possibility of parole for 30 years.

Weeks later, Jesperson was extradited to Washington, where on November 2 he pleaded no contest to the murder of Taujna Bennett. He received another life sentence, again with no chance of parole for 30 years. On November 27, 1995, Laverne Pavlinac and John Sosnovske were released from jail after serving four years in prison for a murder they didn't commit.

Investigators used Jesperson's DNA and other forensic evidence to link him to the murder of Laurie Ann Pentland. Again, the judge in the case sentenced him to life in prison with no chance of parole for 30 years. He was promptly transferred to the Oregon State Penitentiary to begin serving his sentence.

On June 3, 1998, after two years of legal wrangling, the state of Wyoming caved to Jesperson's demands, lifting the death penalty and sentencing him to life in prison for the murder of Angela Subrize. The sentence was made consecutive to his sentences in Washington and Oregon.

He has not yet been charged in any of the other killings to which he has confessed. Jesperson still seeks as much attention as possible, making the news for starting a serial killer pen pal club, then for selling hand-drawn art stamped with a happy face to anyone willing to send him money.

Keith Hunter Jesperson is currently incarcerated at the Oregon State Penitentiary. He will be eligible for parole on March 1, 2063, at the age of 108.

CHAPTER FIVE

Thomas Neill Cream
(1850–1892)

November 16, 1892

THOMAS NEILL CREAM DID NOT SLEEP MUCH THE NIGHT OF November 15, 1892.

Confined to his solitary cell at Newgate Prison in London, England, the former doctor tossed and turned in his bunk, unable to settle. The irony seemed particularly cruel that on this one last night he could not sleep, because in a few hours his rest would be eternal.

When he sat, he held his face in his hands, moaning audibly as the complete realization of what daybreak would bring struck him again and again. He ran his hands often through his rough, thick beard and polished his gold-framed glasses, squinting each time his left eye began rolling inward. Sometimes he shook, praying silently for one last kiss of the opium or low-grain morphine he had bolstered his frayed nerves with over the last several years—ever since the last time he was incarcerated. On the few times he had tried to quit using either drug, he'd at least had the intoxicating taste of alcohol to replace them. Here, inside Newgate, there was no such comfort.

He wasn't sure of the hour, but soon people began to visit his cell, and he knew with total certainty that there was no escape this time.

The prison staff led Cream, bound in shackles, from his cell at the prison to the hangman's room where his fate awaited him.

Public hangings had been stopped in England several years before, in 1868, but that didn't stop people from turning out to the prison anyway. Cream's trial had been sensational. The Scottish-born, Canadian-bred doctor was charged with the murders of four women and the attempted murder of a fifth. Each issue of London's newspapers had carried detailed descriptions of the testimony, as well as drawings of Cream, his lawyer, his fiancée and the one witness who had effectively placed the hangman's noose around his neck. Cream's demise was a foregone conclusion even before the trial began. Few convicted criminals escaped the clutches of Mr. Justice Henry "Hanging" Hawkins.

Cream's trial was one element of closure for an impoverished East London that knew little calm. In an area overrun with music halls, vermin, alcohol and prostitutes, crime was a simple way of life. So too was murder. Four years earlier, the entire country had been shocked to learn of the Whitechapel murders, a string of prostitute killings marked by a demonic escalation of violence. The killer, now dubbed "Jack the Ripper," taunted the press with letters detailing his crimes. His last murder had been the most violent;

he had essentially eviscerated his victim. Then, with no word of warning, the killings stopped. Jack had never been found.

Cream had also preyed on East London's streetwalkers but in a far more insipid way. He preferred poison to physical violence. His position as a doctor gave him access to toxic potions and also engendered a degree of trust in his victims. Although there was little direct evidence linking Cream with each killing, what proof there was was irrefutable. The jury's 10-minute deliberation before finding Cream guilty came with little surprise. What followed, however, was completely unexpected.

Cream shook visibly as the hangman, Mr. Billington, placed Cream on the gallows and placed the noose around his neck. Billington already calculated that by using Cream's height and weight that the prisoner would need to drop five feet to achieve the desired result. Once the noose was affixed, a cloth mask was wrapped around Cream's head, a justice of the peace all the while reminding those few in attendance why they were there.

Billington checked everything one last time before acknowledging that he was ready. He walked over to the side of the gallows and prepared to throw the bar.

It was muffled, barely audible, but those who claimed to hear it never forgot it.

With his last breath, Cream suddenly began to shout, "I am Jack the..."

At that moment, the hatch opened below his feet and he plunged five feet, the noose cleanly snapping his neck.

Outside the prison, a black flag flew in the morning breeze, signalling the execution had been completed. The thousands outside celebrated with cheers and shouts of joy, oblivious to the glaring question mark Dr. Thomas Neill Cream had left on history the second before he died.

East London was not for the faint of heart, but those who lived there had little choice.

The area of Lambeth was already in decline as the Waterloo Bridge, built in 1817, further isolated London's classes from one another. On the far side of the bridge, on the city's outskirts, crime and degeneration reigned. Homes were ripped apart in favour of building tram stations, and the lower class, who already had little in the way of work or lodgings, found their livelihoods further constrained. The slum stank of rotting fish, and the fumes of nearby canneries clogged the air. Dirty children as well as adults hawked wares in the streets, ignoring the rotting corpses of horses and other animals that lay in the roadways unattended.

Distraction in Lambeth, however, was simple. Music halls and pubs offered cheap drinks—and the neighbourhood's streetwalkers offered a few hours of distraction. Prostitution was a necessity for the women who gravitated to the city in search of more than what the countryside offered. They inevitably slipped into the bubbling cauldron of alcohol and opium that dominated Lambeth's society, turning tricks as much to feed their habits as to pay the rent.

Violence was equally prevalent as drunken men took out their frustrations about life on their wives and children after tipping back a few. Screams for help were often ignored because they were so frequent. The only enduring code of conduct revolved around the presence of police officers in the neighbourhood, who were just as likely to end up the victims of an unruly mob as anyone else.

Still, murder was murder, regardless of who the victims were or what they did. The Whitechapel murders in 1888 had terrified and thrilled the masses but equally illustrated how susceptible the lower class was to anyone wishing to indulge their sick fantasies. Few women, however, heeded the murders' implications. The streetwalkers still had to make their money, and the easiest way to do that was to trade themselves for a few shillings behind the Waterloo Bridge.

On October 9, 1891, Eliza Masters, a Lambeth-area prostitute, met up with her friend Elizabeth May to keep an appointment with a gentleman they had met. Three days earlier, the trio had spent the evening in one another's company, visiting several music halls and pubs. The man, who claimed he was once a medical student at St. Thomas Hospital, later sent Masters a note asking to meet both her and May on October 9 for another night of merriment. He also requested she return the letter to him when they met.

It was an odd request, but few of Masters' clients could be classified as normal, so she dutifully packed up the letter, joined up with May and headed out to meet their new friend.

Although Masters and May saw their new friend that night, he never saw them. He was interested in another streetwalker working the area, a young woman named Matilda Clover. Masters and May followed the pair as they made their way to Clover's rooming house on Lambeth Road and disappeared inside. Masters shrugged off the encounter, eventually returning home and destroying the note.

On October 13, Ellen Donworth, a 19-year-old woman who had grown tired of her job labelling bottles and had fled to the streets, left her rooming house for a meeting at the York Hotel on Waterloo Road. At approximately 7:00 PM, a female friend of Donworth's saw her and a man walk together out of a dark court, though the friend didn't get a good look at the man. Minutes later, fruit vendor James Styles saw Donworth stumbling through the street, supporting herself against a wall and looking drunk. She suddenly keeled over onto her face and began writhing on the ground.

Her discomfort, however, had little to do with alcohol. She was in agonizing pain, and no sooner had Styles returned her to her boarding house than she began to convulse. Each seizure grew increasingly violent, frightening her friend and landlady, who had come to tend to her, to the point that they summoned a doctor's assistant, John Johnson, to the home.

"A tall gentleman with cross eyes, a silk hat and bushy whiskers gave me a drink twice out of a bottle with white stuff in it," she managed to croak between gasps of pain. Between her seizures, her pain and her statement, Johnson believed it most likely that she had been poisoned with strychnine. Johnson and the assembled group immediately transferred Donworth to St. Thomas Hospital, but there was little anyone could do. She died on the way.

Two days later, a doctor who performed an autopsy on Donworth confirmed what Johnson had already suspected. After extracting her stomach contents and literally tasting them, the doctor confirmed the bitter flavour of strychnine. She had been poisoned. The incident was promptly reported to the police.

Five days after the autopsy, on October 20, Matilda Clover left her Lambeth Road rooming house. Lucy Rose, a 21-year-old servant girl in the home, found a note from a man asking Clover to meet him outside the Canterbury Music Hall at approximately 7:30 PM. In the letter, the writer also requested that Clover bring the note with her.

Clover was in a rough spot. She was the mother of a young child and had recently thrown the father, Fred, out of their home after a big fight. She was also something of a drinker. Unlike many prostitutes with a similar problem, however, Clover sought help. Every year she paid a few pennies to a society that provided a doctor to local prostitutes. When Clover told the doctor about her drinking problem, he prescribed her a bromide of potassium to help her quit.

Later on the night of October 20, Clover returned to her home in the company of a tall, stocky man with a heavy moustache and gold-rimmed spectacles. Clover was later heard to call out "Good night, Fred," as the man left the home. She stepped out shortly afterwards to grab one last pot of ale before bed, but no one heard her return home. Instead, both Rose and Clover's landlady, Mrs. Vowles, were awoken at 3:00 AM by screams coming from Clover's room. She was lying in bed, convulsing uncontrollably and sobbing in pain.

"That man Fred has poisoned me. He gave me some pills," Clover told the two women.

Vowles and Rose tried to give her tea and milk, but Clover couldn't keep anything down. A doctor's assistant called to the scene was convinced Clover was drunk, gave her some medicine and left. Shortly afterwards, her face turned black. Matilda Clover died at approximately 9:00 AM.

No one, however, was willing to believe what had in effect been her last words. Instead, the doctors who took one quick look at her corpse inferred she had combined her bromide of potassium with her regular brandy, a medical no-no that could easily result in death. No autopsy was performed. Clover was buried on October 27 in a pauper's grave with more than a dozen other coffins in Tooting Cemetery.

On April 11, 1892, Constable George Comley was
on patrol in Lambeth at approximately 2:30 AM when
he saw a man with a moustache, gold-rimmed glasses
and dark overcoat leave a boarding house in the area.
At the time he thought nothing of it. Approximately
one hour later, a horse-drawn cab came clattering to
a stop outside the same house, called by the landlady
to take the two women to the hospital. Comley could
hear screams coming from inside. He followed the
cabman into the house and found two young women,
Alice Marsh, 21, and Emma Shrivell, 18, lying on the
floor in their nightgowns, writhing in pain and convulsing violently. Their landlady, Charlotte Vogt, had
overheard their screams and come running. Alice was
already foaming at the mouth while Emma convulsed
on the floor.

Before they left in the cab, Marsh and Shrivell, a pair
of prostitutes who had originally come to London
to be actresses, explained that they had entertained
a gentleman in their room and treated him to a dinner of canned salmon and beer. In exchange, he gave
each of the women three pills, explaining that he was
a doctor and that the pills would help improve their
complexions.

Alice did not survive the trip to the hospital. Emma
was given chloroform by the house surgeon but died
six hours later.

At first, both the doctors and the police wondered if
the women had eaten a bad tin of salmon. A search of
the apartment, however, turned up a few suspicious

items. The salmon can was of an unusual brand not commonly sold in the area. Police also found a burned postcard in the fireplace, cancelling an April 11 meeting. There was no signature.

The doctors now strongly suspected that poison might be involved. Their stomach contents were removed, mashed, filtered and tested, by colour, alkaloid content and taste. The purple colour of the stomach remains and the bitter flavour confirmed the presence of strychnine. Further testing revealed that Marsh had ingested six and three-quarter grains of the poison, whereas Shrivell had consumed three grains. One grain of strychnine was generally considered to be a fatal dose.

Within two weeks of their deaths, someone posted letters from around London, either offering information on the murders in exchange for money or trying to blackmail other parties. On April 26, Dr. Joseph Harper received a letter in which the writer offered to destroy evidence that implicated Harper's son, Walter—a promising intern at St. Thomas Hospital— in the murder in exchange for 1500 pounds. It was signed W. H. Murray. Harper responded through a personal ad in the *Daily Chronicle*, but nothing ever came of it.

The letters didn't stop there. Assistant coroner George Percival received a letter from the same person saying the writer had evidence, also implicating Walter Harper, which he had picked up from an American detective.

Both letters, in fact, were the continuation of a black-mail scheme that had begun the previous fall. In October 1891, the East Surrey deputy coroner received a letter from an A. O'Brien claiming he could name Ellen Donworth's murderer in exchange for 300,000 pounds. One month later, recently elected Member of Parliament Frederick Smith, who also worked as a bookseller, received a letter from an H. Bayne. Bayne stated he had evidence implicating Smith in Don-worth's murder. Smith was supposed to respond by posting a poster in his store window calling for a meet-ing. Smith, at the police's urging, did so. No one ever made contact.

The police also received a letter saying Smith was responsible, but they had no idea who this Bayne per-son was. They were further stumped on November 30 when Dr. William Broadbent, a physician at St. Mary's Hospital, received a letter in which the writer claimed to be in possession of evidence that proved Broadbent had killed Matilda Clover with strychnine. The evi-dence could be easily disposed of for 2500 pounds.

Broadbent contacted the police, who suggested he follow through with the writer's demand to place an ad in the *Chronicle* requesting a meeting. The police watched Broadbent's house for days but never saw anyone the least bit suspicious. It was considered an odd development, because the only Matilda Clover who had died recently had passed away because she drank too much.

The Marsh and Shrivell murders, however, convinced the police they had a larger problem on their
hands. Officers fanned out through the streets, interviewing all the chemists in the area to try to find out
who might have recently purchased large quantities
of strychnine. Anyone declaring themselves a doctor of
any sort could purchase whatever amount they
wanted, provided the transaction was logged. The
search initially turned up little.

On May 6, the police exhumed Matilda Clover's
corpse from its pauper's grave, sifting through 14 other
coffins before they finally located hers. The autopsy
took three weeks, at the end of which one-sixteenth of
a grain of strychnine was found in her digestive tract.
After emulsifying the contents and confirming the bitter taste of the poison, a doctor injected a frog with the
mixture. It died 15 minutes later.

That same month, the police received information
that pointed them to their best suspect. The break,
however, did not come from old-fashioned police
work or witness accounts. It came from the killer
himself. A man named Thomas Neill Cream had
befriended John Haynes, a former police detective
who was now an out-of-work engineer. The pair had
met at a photographer's house and began spending
almost every day together. During one such meeting
at a nearby music hall, Cream admitted to his new
friend that he knew three other prostitutes who had
been murdered—their names were Ellen Donworth,
Matilda Clover and a woman named Lou Harvey.

Cream even went so far as to take Haynes by Clover and Harvey's homes.

Ever the detective, even though he no longer worked as one, Haynes made his own inquiries and discovered that Clover had died of drink and was not a victim of murder. And despite his best efforts, he could not find anyone named Lou Harvey.

On May 12, three weeks after Haynes and Cream last met, Constable Comley, the same man who had been on patrol the night Marsh and Shrivell had died, saw a man eyeing several prostitutes outside the Canterbury Music Hall. He realized that the man looked an awful lot like the man he had seen coming out of Marsh and Shrivell's home the night they died. After reporting the encounter to his sergeant, Comley became one of several officers who placed the man, identified later as Cream, under surveillance.

Haynes continued to press Cream for more information on the murders, and the suspect was more than happy to oblige. It turned out that Cream lodged in the same building as Walter Harper, the young intern who an anonymous letter writer had repeatedly stated was responsible for Donworth's death. Haynes relayed the information to his police contacts at Scotland Yard. Cream seemed to know more about the killings than any other person, even those connected with the investigation. At the time, investigators were still waiting for the results of Clover's autopsy and could not locate any woman named Lou Harvey. Cream seemed as likely a suspect as anyone.

The only other suspect they had was a phantom named Fred. Investigators had succeeded in tracking down Lucy Rose, the servant girl who described Clover's final hours and her shouting out, "Good night, Fred." It turned out the other three victims had also known a man named Fred. Given the time that elapsed between the Clover and Marsh–Shrivell murders, the police thought Fred might be a seaman who spent long periods of time at sea and murdered only when he returned to land. Cream's increasingly strange behaviour, however, soon supplanted any idea of Fred as a suspect. On June 18, Scotland Yard sent Inspector Frederick Jarvis to North America to learn more about this American doctor named Thomas Cream.

They inevitably found a lot more than they had been initially looking for.

Thomas Neill Cream was born on May 27, 1850, in Glasgow, Scotland, to William and Mary Cream (née Elder). Shortly after Thomas' birth, the family left Scotland for the British colony of Canada. There the family settled in Wolfe's Cove, Québec, where William became the manager of a lumber and shipbuilding yard. William eventually broke off on his own to start up his own successful lumber wholesale business, the Cream Lumber Mill.

At first it seemed Thomas would follow in his father's footsteps, beginning an apprenticeship in shipbuilding at an early age. In 1872, however, with his father paying the way, Thomas instead enrolled at McGill University in Montréal and studied medicine. Cream spent his school years studying and his summers working for his father. Thomas' classmates were always struck by his fine clothes and ostentatious jewellery—and his drinking ability.

An event in month of his graduation in March 1876 turned out to be something of a scandalous affair. In his final year, Cream's home at 106 Mansfield in Montréal caught fire. Although it was never confirmed, it was widely suspected that Cream had set fire to the building to cash in on the $350 insurance money.

Seven months later, Cream, now 26, found himself staring down the barrel of a rifle and marching to the wedding altar. He had been engaged to Flora Eliza Brooks, the daughter of a Waterloo hotel owner named Lyman Brooks. In September 1876, Flora became ill and went to the doctor. The physician promptly informed her father that Flora had recently had an abortion. Brooks wasted little time in escorting the groom to the altar at gunpoint. The following day, Cream left his new wife, snuck out of his home and sailed to London, England.

Cream's fortunes in England were not much better than they were in Canada. He worked as an obstetrics intern at St. Thomas Hospital but failed the admissions exam to become a member of the Royal College of Surgeons. He was, however, admitted to the Royal College of Physicians and Surgeons in Edinburgh and was qualified as a male midwife.

His marriage didn't stop him from wooing the women of London, both women of stature and street-walkers. His marital status, though, changed abruptly in May 1877 when Flora, who was still in Canada, again became ill. She told her doctor she had been taking some pills that her husband sent her in the mail. The doctor advised her to stop taking the pills. She died soon afterwards, and Cream collected $200 from her father as part of an inheritance.

A year later in May 1878, Cream returned to Canada and set up a doctor's office in London, Ontario. The office, located above Bennett's Clothing Store, soon became a source of rumour, because streetwalkers let it be known to their fellow prostitutes that the doctor was providing abortions, which were illegal at the time. The scandal came to a head on May 3, 1879, when a little girl found the body of Kate Hutchinson behind Cream's office. Her corpse reeked of chloroform, and she had scratches on her face.

At the subsequent coroner's inquest, Kate's roommate testified that Kate had recently become pregnant by a man to whom she was not married and had gone to Cream's office for an abortion, for which he charged her $100. As suspect as the situation was, the inquest did not find enough evidence to say Cream had somehow caused Hutchinson's death, despite the scratch marks on her face.

His reputation tarnished, Cream fled south of the border and set up shop in Chicago, where he continued to offer abortions to local women and prostitutes.

There were 3500 prostitutes in Chicago's population of 800,000 at the time, some of whom used Cream's services. He was assisted in his duties by a midwife named Hattie Mack, a black woman.

On Friday, August 20, 1880, the body of Mary Anne Faulkner was found rotting in Mack's boarding room in Chicago. The Ottawa-born woman had apparently come to Chicago for an abortion, but something went wrong during the procedure. Witnesses told the police they saw a man matching Cream's description leaving Mack's apartment one evening. The police also found a letter from Mack to Cream in which she told him she was leaving because Faulkner had died.

The police later tracked down and arrested Mack, who told the police Cream had told her to hide Faulkner in her home. Cream blamed Mack, saying the midwife had started the abortion before he got to her room and that he had tried to save the woman's life. Ultimately, Cream was indicted for murder and held in custody until his trial.

The trial, which began on November 16, 1880, was a laughable affair. The U.S. Civil War was still a recent memory, and though the country's African American slaves had been emancipated, there was no such thing as racial equality. Cream's lawyer effectively focused the jury's attention on his client's upstanding reputation as a schooled, white doctor. Who were they to believe, defence counsel Alfred Trude asked, a white doctor or a black midwife? The jury chose to believe the white doctor, deliberating for less than 15 minutes before finding Cream not guilty.

Cream, however, was back in court within a matter of years, again defending himself against a charge of murder. In February 1881, a woman named Julia Stott visited his Chicago office to purchase an epilepsy antidote for her husband, Daniel. Cream himself had created and marketed the medication. Daniel died shortly after taking the antidote. Cream responded quickly, telegraphing the coroner's office and suggesting the druggist who prepared the medicine had used too much strychnine. Cream even offered to sue the company for damages on Julia Stott's behalf.

The police didn't believe his story. An autopsy revealed Stott had consumed three times the fatal dose of strychnine. Already on bail for trying to blackmail a man who had reneged on his doctor's bill, Cream again fled to Canada, but he was arrested in July 1881 and ordered to stand trial for one count of murder in the death of Daniel Stott.

During the September trial in Chicago, Julia Stott turned State's evidence and told the court she and Cream had fallen in love and that he had hatched a plan to poison Daniel, then sue the drug manufacturer. She told the jury she saw Cream tamper with the pills right before her husband had taken the medicine and died.

It was all the jury needed. On September 23, Cream was found guilty of murder and sentenced to life in prison at the Illinois State Penitentiary in Joliet.

The prison system of the 1880s was one of the most seething sources of corruption in all of the United States. Money could buy anything from comfort to privilege to release. As it stood, Cream's stay in Joliet rounded out at approximately 10 years. He was released in 1891 after his brother Daniel "convinced" Governor Joseph W. Fifer to grant him executive clemency. The convincing came at the same time that William Cream died, leaving the son he had disowned in 1881 the sum of $16,000.

The Thomas Neill Cream who came out of prison was not the same man who had gone in. This new man was more dishevelled, owlier and had a predilection for strange behaviour and drug use. After a short stay with his brother and sister-in-law in Canada, the family suggested Thomas take a trip to England. He agreed and spent most of the transoceanic voyage drunk out of his mind.

Since Cream's return to London, the police had discerned a few things about him. He had spent most of his time reading and writing in his room or frequenting the company of prostitutes. He enjoyed using both opium and low-grain morphine.

By tracing Cream's movements upon his return, the police learned he had purchased a product known as nux vomica, a medicinal mixture of bromide and strychnine, on October 12, as well as several gelatin capsules. He introduced himself to people as Thomas Neill, M.D. He successfully courted Laura Sabbatini in

November and bankrolled her dressmaking ambitions. Cream proposed by the end of the month, then disappeared back to Canada in January to attend to some unfinished business with his father's estate. On his way home, he made a quick stop in New York, where he ordered 500 one-sixteenth grain strychnine capsules and then returned to England, landing in Liverpool on April 2.

At first, the police were convinced that Cream was at least a blackmailer, but his role as a murderer seemed sketchy at best. Even with little hard evidence, the police arrested Cream on June 3 on charges of blackmail. Their ultimate goal was to buy themselves more time to collect more evidence.

The evidence came in spades. On June 17, Eliza Masters and Elizabeth May informed the police that Cream was the one and the same man they had seen going into Matilda Clover's home the previous October. It was enough for the police to begin an inquest into Clover's death, which convened on June 22.

Hundreds of spectators watched the proceedings, which were stacked against Cream from the very start. The Crown produced several witnesses, who each framed some small part of the story. A druggist testified that he had sold Cream the nux vomica mixture, and a police officer produced a handwritten list, found in Cream's home, of each of the poisoning victims and their date of death.

The most dramatic moment, however, came when Lou Harvey—the prostitute Cream claimed had died but no one could find—took the stand to testify. Her real name was Louisa Harris. She told the inquest she had met Cream on October 22 of the previous year at the Alhambra Theatre, and they had spent the night together at the Palace Hotel. They also met the next night on the embankment of the Thames River, at which time Cream presented her with a couple of figs and some pills, which he said would help her complexion. With Cream watching intently, Harris had pretended to swallow the pills, then threw them down the embankment when Cream turned his back. Although they had plans to attend the Oxford Music Hall, Cream suddenly explained he had to return to the hospital and would be unable to go. He told Harris he would meet her later on in the evening. He never showed.

Harris also told the court that she and Cream had run into each other again three weeks later in a music hall. When Harris reminded Cream who she was, he acted surprised, then walked away and spent the rest of the evening on the far end of the hall.

On July 13, the inquest concluded that Cream was most likely responsible for Clover's murder. Five days later, Cream was charged with the murders of Donworth, Clover, Marsh and Shrivell, as well as the attempted murder of Louisa Harris. The press sensationalized the four-day trial in October as the "Lambeth poisoning mystery," and the case opened to a packed and rapt audience in London's Old Bailey.

Cream must have known he had little chance of beating the charges. The judge, Mr. Justice Henry

Hawkins, was known in the legal community as "Hanging Hawkins" for his propensity for sentencing defendants to hang. Although Cream's counsel, Gerald Geoghegan, was a well-respected lawyer, the judicial system did not allow him to mount a vigorous defence. Cream himself was not allowed to take the stand to try to refute the evidence against him. The Crown called many of the same witnesses it had during the inquest, including Louisa Harris. Geoghegan called no witnesses, instead arguing before the judge and jury that none of the witnesses could put his client at any of the murder scenes.

It wasn't enough. In less than 10 minutes, the jury returned a verdict of guilty. Hawkins held true to his nickname and ordered Cream to hang in three Sundays' time. He said the murders were "...so diabolical in [their] character, fraught with so much cold-blooded cruelty, [they] could be expiated only by your death."

Cream's execution was ultimately delayed by one week while his lawyer worked to convince the Home Secretary that Cream had been insane at the time of the murders—that his ability to reason between right and wrong were destroyed by years of opium and morphine use. His lawyer tracked down numerous witnesses, many of whom had travelled on the same boat as Cream during his trips to North America to testify about his seemingly unbalanced mental state. The Secretary of State, however, declined the application for clemency.

On November 16, a crowd of several thousand gathered outside the Newgate Prison in anticipation of Cream's execution. Inside, Cream was fitted with a noose, had his face covered in a mask and was read his death warrant.

According to witnesses present at the affair, Cream began to shout "I am Jack the..." just as his body fell through the gallows.

Between August and November of 1888, a man known in history as Jack the Ripper killed five London prostitutes within a one-kilometre area of the city. The name "Jack the Ripper" was given to the killer because of a letter sent to the Central News Agency that was signed with the name.

The killings of Mary Ann Nichols, Annie Chapman, Elizabeth Stride, Catharine Eddowes and Mary Jane Kelly were noteworthy for their sensational brutality. In almost every case, the woman was first strangled and then her throat was slit. The body was then mutilated with an animal-like frenzy that increased with every killing. After Kelly's murder in November 1888, the murders suddenly stopped. Jack the Ripper was never caught.

Trying to figure out who Jack the Ripper was is a hobby for many. Called "Ripperologists," these weekend detectives across the world all have their own theories as to the identity of the murderer.

Given Cream's last statement, it was inevitable that some Ripperologists would focus on Cream as a possible suspect. Some have gone so far as to compare Cream's handwriting with the Ripper letters and to declare the two very similar.

Cream's final words, if true, certainly lend credence to the letter theory. Examining the evidence, however, it is increasingly unlikely Cream could have also been the Whitechapel murderer.

The most significant argument against him revolves around the fact that he was in jail in Illinois in 1888 at the time of the Whitechapel killings. If he was in jail, it seems consequently difficult that he could have somehow made his way to London, England, to participate in a violent frenzy of serial murder. This most blatant of facts has not stopped some Ripperologists from considering Cream as a suspect. Some argue Cream might have been released earlier than 1891, which could have put him back in London in time. Others argue that a Cream "body double," with whom the doctor worked in tandem in his criminal life, could have been the killer—one serving sentences while the other committed murder. Perhaps Cream or the body double committed the Ripper murders while the other was imprisoned in Joliet.

That argument also explains the other large discrepancy in the case: the modus operandi. Thomas Neill Cream was a poisoner, a man who could not even bring himself to kill with his own bare hands, let alone watch the women he poisoned die with his own eyes. The killings were cold, calculated and removed. The Whitechapel murders, however, were violent, sexual and sadistic, up close and personal. The Ripper murders took place before the Lambeth poisonings. Research shows that serial killers become increasingly violent with each new killing, not less. Consequently, Cream could not have been Jack the Ripper because his modus operandi was too different.

Nevertheless, Ripperologists argue that if Cream did in fact have a body double, it could explain the two markedly different serial murder strings. One may have preferred poisoning and the other gratuitous violence. Perhaps the body double committed the Ripper murders while Cream was in prison, indulging in his own sick fantasies before Cream was freed and indulged his own.

The evidence seems to dispute the idea, especially considering that the poisonings stopped after Cream's execution and the Ripper never reappeared.

Still, like all conspiracy theories, Cream's profile as a Whitechapel suspect will likely endure.

CHAPTER SIX

John Martin Crawford
(1962–)

IN THE BUSHES JUST OUTSIDE BARE ASS BEACH, 20 MINUTES south of Saskatoon, Saskatchewan, Bill Corrigan sat in the car and waited for his friend to return.

It was a late spring night in 1992, and the sun had already disappeared behind Saskatchewan's endless horizon. The sky above was clear, but Corrigan wasn't watching the stars or the moon, wasn't contemplating his role in the universe or the celestial wonders of outer space. Instead, he drank a can of Pilsner beer, smoked a cigarette and waited.

No, Bill Corrigan had long ago given up wondering what the world held in store for him. His place in life was effectively cemented by the 50 entries on his criminal record, a litany of robberies, thefts and other violations too numerous to mention. He had recently finished a 10-year stint at the Saskatchewan Penitentiary in Prince Albert for a store robbery. It was during that stint that he had met his friend, the man who he had spent the night with and even now waited for near the shores of the South Saskatchewan River.

The night had started off like any other night, his friend picking Corrigan up from the cheap, seedy

Saskatoon motel Corrigan called home. The pair had
cruised in his friend's mother's green Chevy Nova,
driving up and down the streets, checking out hookers and other women who might be easy. Most of
the prostitutes knew the pair on sight, but they knew
Corrigan's companion more than they knew Corrigan himself. His friend was known as a "bad trick,"
a guy who got rough with the girls and who didn't
always pay what he had promised. Still, it was never
hard to find someone willing to take a drive.

As they drove, Corrigan had watched his friend
shoot up another needle full of Ritalin, and they eventually found a girl wandering behind the Albany
Hotel. She was young—looked to still be a teenager
and an Indian, which was how his friend liked his
girls. They'd seen her around the area quite a bit. She
needed a ride somewhere and said she wanted to
party. Bill's friend told her to hop in.

Corrigan tapped cigarette ash out the window and
pulled on his beer again, trying to remember her
name. *Angie*, he thought. *Yeah, Angie*.

They gave her a ride to a house in Saskatoon, but she
came back out and joined them in the car, and Corrigan's friend had driven them back here, out on Bare Ass
Beach where young kids liked to come to party and
swim naked in the river. The evening started off like
any other night. The three of them smoked and drank
beer in the car, mostly just talking. After a few minutes,
Corrigan's friend told him to take a walk. That was
always the cue that he was ready to go, so Corrigan,

thinking nothing of it because it had happened so many times before, stepped out of the car and wandered a short distance away, waiting for him to finish.

What came next, however, was not normal for their evenings. Corrigan heard his friend yelling at Angie, heard her screaming, heard the muffled thumps of fist striking skin. The car door opened and Corrigan watched his friend roughly grab the nearly naked girl, hauling her into the bushes and screaming at the top of his lungs.

And so Corrigan got back in the car and waited for his friend to come back with her.

Then he suddenly paused, and a tremour of fear ran through his veins.

He didn't give me back my knife.

Suddenly, Corrigan couldn't hear anything.

Fighting a growing sense of dread, he exited the car and made his way into the bushes. He'd walked no more than 30 metres when he saw his friend standing over Angie. She was lying on the ground, and Corrigan instantly recognized the hilt of his hunting knife protruding from her stomach. There were a dozen other puncture wounds on her body. She was obviously dead.

"What did you do?" Bill Corrigan stammered to his friend, John Martin Crawford.

Crawford didn't respond, just asked Corrigan to help cover her up. They had to hurry. Crawford had to have his mom's car back home by 9:00 PM.

Later that night, as Corrigan watched Crawford soak his precious hunting knife in mouthwash, Bill began to wonder. A lifetime of living on the edge of society had brought him little more than jail time to this point. And now he had just watched his friend kill a young girl.

No one in that car was a saint. But that didn't mean that anyone deserved to die.

Crawford dropped Corrigan off at the hotel that night, warning him to keep his mouth shut. While Corrigan smoked alone in his hotel room, he wondered what he was going to do.

October 1994

No animal that lives in Saskatchewan has a skull that resembles that of a human being. So there was no question of what was found when Dr. Ernie Walker, a professor of anthropology at the University of Saskatchewan, arrived at the site near Bare Ass Beach.

The police had called him in a few days before. A hunter prowling the area had come across the human skull lying in the dirt. Police had already attended the scene—as had the press—and they were now asking for Walker's opinion.

That it was human, there was no doubt. The police often responded to reports of bones and decaying remains found in the wild. More often than not the bones were those of an animal, some of which can be difficult to distinguish from human remains.

In those cases in which the remains are identified as human, they are often remains of an archaeological nature. The First Nations people of Canada had lived in the area for thousands of years, and their burial sites dotted the province. Walker instantly knew, however, that this was no archaeological find. The remains were not only human but were also relatively fresh.

As crews excavated more of the body, they recovered not just bones, but also hair and other soft tissue, matter that would have decayed into the soil long ago if this was indeed an ancient burial plot. After a full day of work, Walker and the RCMP crews working with him had recovered 90 percent of the skeleton from a relatively wide area. Some of the bones showed signs of damage, indicating that other animals in the area had preyed on the body at some point. The corpse had obviously not been buried.

With the skeleton now in his lab, Walker was able to reconstruct the skeleton and eventually make some deductions based on the condition of the bones before him. He hypothesized that the skeleton was that of a woman, most likely of First Nations descent, who had died sometime in her early 20s. That was as close as Walker could get in terms of an identity.

Within days, Walker found himself again at work in the same area. On October 21, 1994, an RCMP constable walking through the area came across a human skull protruding out of the dirt only a few dozen metres from the site of the first skeleton. When crews

descended on the area to excavate it, they also deliberately searched the surrounding area for more
remains or clues. Investigators began to worry that
they had stumbled upon a human dumping ground.
Searching the area grid by grid, crews poked and prodded the earth to see what else they could find. Only
50 metres away, they found a third skull.

The second and third skeletons, however, differed
in both their condition and how they'd been disposed.
The second skeleton had also been dumped in the
area with little effort made to bury it. Crews were able
to excavate 85 percent of the body, and the police
shipped it to Walker's lab for further analysis. His preliminary findings were sobering: the skeleton was that
of a girl, probably of First Nations descent, who had
died in her late teens.

The third skeleton was the freshest of the three,
with significant soft tissue remaining, meaning the
victim had been killed more recently than the other
two. This person had been trussed up with an extension cord, wrapped in a blanket and buried in a shallow grave. Forensic scientists examining the body
used larvae of the black blowfly, common to Saskatchewan, to determine that the body had been dumped
in the area sometime the previous spring.

During a post-mortem medical exam, Walker concluded that the body was that of a woman, also of
First Nations descent, most likely between the ages
of 29 and 32. X-rays revealed she had suffered a broken
jaw and one broken rib. The most macabre discovery

was painfully obvious from the moment the body was unwrapped: the woman's left arm had been sawed off just above the elbow.

In most homicide investigations, the very first—and often most important—step is to identify the victim. But in this case, members of the General Investigation Section (GIS) for Saskatoon had little to go on in this case. Two of the remains were little more than skeletons, and the third was so decomposed that there was no way to tell what the woman might have looked like before she had died. Police found no wallets, no ID and no personal effects near the bodies that could help them in their search for an identity.

The press had already been informed of the discoveries and had even been directed to the dumping ground during the recovery of the last two skeletons. The RCMP admitted they were stumped, that they had no leads as to who these three women were and even less of an idea as to who might have killed them.

The RCMP, however, were lying.

July 1993

Corporal Stan Lintick of the Customs and Excise unit was on vacation when one of his snitches called.

Bill Corrigan, a con with a history of theft, robberies, and break and enters, had been working for Lintick for quite some time now, passing on information about cigarette smuggling over the border between Saskatchewan and the U.S. On this particular day, however, Corrigan's information had little to do with cigarettes. He wanted to talk about murder,

With Lintick away, the job of interviewing Corrigan fell to Constable Malcolm Eskelson, who questioned the snitch in his police car. According to reporter Warren Goulding's book, *Just Another Indian: A Serial Killer and Canada's Indifference*, it was at this time that the name John Martin Crawford first came to the attention of police.

In speaking with Eskelson, Corrigan said he had information about the murder of a girl named Angie, and that two men—Crawford and a man named John Potter—had been responsible. Corrigan and Eskelson drove out to the supposed dump site south of Saskatoon, but apparently they didn't even bother getting out of the car. Corrigan admitted that he and Crawford had hung out with Angie before, but he had not been involved in the murder.

Corrigan's story was far from believable at the time. Although he was a valuable snitch for Customs and Excise, his reputation as a con and as a human being was not beyond reproach. When Eskelson first began investigating Corrigan's allegation, he found no trace of anyone answering to the name of John Potter.

When Lintick returned from vacation, he contacted Corrigan to follow up on his story. Corrigan maintained there was such a person as John Potter. He also said there might be more than one body.

On a whim, Lintick borrowed a dog handler and a police dog from the Prince Albert RCMP detachment on August 5, 1993, and searched the area. The dog's highly trained nose turned up nothing. Over the next 14 months, Lintick would return to the area around Bare Ass Beach and wander around, looking for any sign to verify Corrigan's story, but he always came up empty-handed.

One year and two months later, the first skeleton was unearthed in the area. Having never forgotten Corrigan's information, Lintick immediately tracked down his snitch, who was now working as a crossing guard in Winnipeg. Accompanied by GIS Constable Al Keller, Lintick picked up Corrigan at his home and took him back to a Winnipeg hotel for questioning.

Keller spent several hours peppering Corrigan with questions, slowly breaking down Corrigan's initial story and establishing a rapport with the repeat convict. While most of Winnipeg turned into bed that night, Corrigan finally began to sing. He admitted to a far-from-surprised Keller that there was no John Potter, and he agreed to make a recorded statement.

The next day, Corrigan accompanied the pair of detectives to RCMP headquarters in Winnipeg and gave a second statement. Corrigan explained how his former friend, John Martin Crawford, was responsible for the death of at least one, if not more, of the women found near Bare Ass Beach.

It was the best the RCMP could do, but they decided to run with the information they had. On October 11, 1994, police received permission to deploy the Special "O" squad to conduct surveillance of their suspect.

By that night, the special watchers were in place, eyeing the man suspected of the murder of a woman known as Angie.

The speed of the decision to keep tabs on Crawford, however, was only partially linked to the discovery of the bodies. In conducting their background research into Crawford's past, the police came across a fact that could not possibly be ignored.

Crawford had killed before.

John Martin Crawford was born in Steinbach, Manitoba, on March 29, 1962. His parents, Victoria and Al Crawford, did not marry until John was two years old.

John's home life was far from happy. The eldest of three kids, Crawford grew up in a home dominated by a hard-drinking father who worked as a taxi driver and a mother who was addicted to bingo. According to psychological reports filed with the courts, two different babysitters had sexually assaulted Crawford—once when he was four and another at age seven. At the age of four, he was rushed to hospital after suffering severe burns from playing with a cigarette lighter.

As Crawford aged, it became painfully obvious to everyone around him that he was not blessed with the sharpest mental faculties. He failed grade one and was labelled early on as "stupid." By the time he was 12 years old, John was already bullying the smaller kids at school and sniffing glue. As he reached puberty, he moved past glue to marijuana, LSD, magic mushrooms,

Ritalin and Valium. He also drank heavily, stole cars and fought with police. John grew up believing that sex was a service provided by women for a fee.

By age 16, he said he was hearing voices and hallucinating. He was admitted to hospitals and psychiatric wards, where doctors shot off mixed diagnoses of "hebephrenic schizophrenia" and inoculated Crawford with powerful antipsychotic drugs. Sometimes he took them and sometimes he didn't. Although the hallucinations eventually went away, Crawford never stopped drinking, never stopped doing drugs and never stopped believing in his twisted perspective on the roles of men and women.

On Christmas Eve 1981, police in Lethbridge, Alberta, received a tip from a homeless man: he had found the body of a woman behind the old fire hall. Investigators who responded to the scene knew immediately they were dealing with a homicide. They could clearly see the bruises on her face and the deep bite marks that covered her face and breasts. The autopsy revealed she had choked to death on her own vomit. A bruise on her abdomen matched the outline of the brick that was found near her body.

Lethbridge police quickly identified the body as that of Mary Jane Serloin, a woman of First Nations descent originally from the Peigan Reserve, located near Fort McLeod, Alberta. By backtracking her movements the night before, police established that Serloin was last seen drinking in the company of a man at the Bridge Inn in Lethbridge. Witnesses at the inn saw the pair leave the bar around 10:00 PM; the man had returned to the bar alone around midnight.

Eight hours after finding Serloin's body, police went to the home of Victoria and Al Crawford and arrested their 19-year-old son, John. Shortly after his arrest, Crawford agreed to allow police to make a wax mould of his teeth. His dentition matched perfectly the bite marks found on Serloin's body. The bite marks indicated the attack had been sexual in nature, so police charged Crawford with one count of first-degree murder.

Six months later, Crawford appeared in Lethbridge court and entered a plea of guilty to one count of manslaughter in Serloin's death. He had been in custody since the day police arrested him and, by entering the plea, was now guaranteed an even longer period of incarceration. Under the Criminal Code of Canada, the maximum sentence on a charge of manslaughter is life in prison. There is no minimum sentence.

In his judgment, Justice L. D. MacLean noted the violence of the murder as well as Crawford's apparent disregard for his actions by simply returning to the bar for another drink after he had caused Serloin's death. MacLean, in passing the sentence, accepted Crawford's lawyer's argument of his client's deficient mental state and ordered Crawford jailed for 10 years.

Crawford's time in prison was dominated by his deteriorating mental health. He was repeatedly transferred from jail to psychiatric institutions as his hallucinations returned. According to Goulding's book,

Crawford claimed he had ESP. He giggled at inappro-
priate times, spoke in gibberish and stared off into the
distance for long periods of time. On one occasion,
Crawford slashed his own wrist.

Crawford was paroled in 1987 after six years in jail
(two-thirds of his sentence) but was quickly returned
to jail in Drumheller for violating the conditions of his
parole. Despite a psychiatrist's report questioning
whether or not he was able to reintegrate into society,
Corrections Canada again released him from prison in
1989. He went to Saskatoon to live with his mother,
who had moved there to run a group home and who
had also recently divorced Crawford's father.

Crawford took nothing away from his earlier experience in prison. He continued drinking, sniffing
solvents and using illegal drugs. At night, he cruised
Saskatoon's streets in his mother's car. In December
1990, Crawford was arrested and fined $250 for solic-
iting an undercover police officer. Victoria came down
hard on her 28-year-old son, imposing a 9:00 PM curfew.

On May 9, 1992, Janet Sylvestre, a 35-year-old
mother of two, accused Crawford of raping her in
a house just across the street from his mother's group
home. Crawford languished in jail for a month before
he was finally bailed by his mother. Sylvestre, however, did not show up for the trial, and the Crown was
forced to stay the charge for lack of evidence.

On August 7 of the same year, police found an almost
naked Crawford at Bare Ass Beach, wearing only a T-
shirt. They noticed that he seemed to have a very high

fever, so they took him to St. Paul's Hospital. Although at one point Crawford was declared dead, doctors were able to revive him. Upon discharge, Crawford voluntarily entered a detox program but was discharged after four days. Over the next three months, he stayed at two more detox centres but never made any progress. He picked fights with other residents, quarrelled with staff and showed little interest in actually confronting his alcohol and drug demons.

Police again arrested Crawford in October, this time for severely beating a man in Saskatoon after the man refused to give Crawford a cigarette. Crawford was initially charged with attempted murder, but the Crown downgraded the charge to aggravated assault. He was convicted and sentenced to one year in jail.

Upon his release, Crawford was as dangerous as he had ever been. He had received no effective counselling while in prison and returned to live with his mother in a group home populated by the mentally ill and by ex-cons. He had no job and a mother who let him do as he pleased, as long as he had the car home by 9:00 PM.

The first two nights of Special O's surveillance of John Martin Crawford proved to be one of the most contentious parts of the investigation.

On October 11, 1994, officers from the special watchdog task force descended on Victoria Crawford's group home, keeping an eye out for their target. Later that evening, Crawford left the house, hopped into his mother's car and drove away. The watchers followed him.

At around 8:00 PM, the police tracked Crawford as he picked up a visibly drunk Native woman and drove her to a nearby storage lot. The surveillance squad parked close by and watched. Minutes later, officers saw Crawford drive off, and the woman lurched out into the open. Her eyes and nose were swollen, her pants were open, and she was bleeding. The press would later learn that, despite the fact some sort of assault had occurred, the RCMP watchers keeping tabs on Crawford had done nothing to intervene.

When asked if she'd been raped, the woman, who was later identified as Theresa Kematch, denied it. The officer on scene arrested Kematch for being drunk in public and lodged her in cells overnight. She refused to change her story, so the police had no option but to release her later the next day.

The members of Special O again spent the next evening following Crawford around as he drove from street to street, making his usual rounds within the same eight-block radius. Surprisingly, however, Crawford turned in early, well before his 9:00 PM curfew.

Convinced that their quarry was hunkered down for the evening, the on-scene commander called off the surveillance for the night.

The following day, an old man walking his dog 15 kilometres west of Saskatoon came across the body of a woman. She had been badly beaten and was found with a plastic bag over her head. Police later identified her as Janet Sylvestre, 37, the same woman who had accused John Martin Crawford of rape in May 1992.

Eight days later, the second and third skeletons were found.

The police combined the investigation of Sylvestre's murder with that of the three sets of remains. They were able to find a couple of witnesses—prostitutes who claimed that a man matching the description of a friend of Crawford's had jumped out of a grey Cougar and pulled Sylvestre into the car.

Investigators took the information under advisement and continued their surveillance of Crawford. Although they were waiting for him to somehow incriminate himself during the operation, police had another card that had yet to be played. Police at Saskatoon's F Division headquarters had negotiated an agreement with Crawford's old drinking buddy, Bill Corrigan. In exchange for $15,000 split up over two payments, Corrigan agreed to cooperate with police and testify at any court proceedings against Crawford.

In mid-November, the police released sketches of two of the three women whose remains were found near Bare Ass Beach. Each sketch was effectively a reconstruction of what the women would have looked like when they were alive. By this time investigators already knew the name of the third victim who had been found wrapped in the blanket. She was Eva Taysup, originally from the Yellow Quill First Nation in Saskatchewan, and she had four children.

In mid-December, a man informed police that he had not heard from his friend Shelley Napope for quite some time, and that she closely resembled one of the sketches. Through dental records, police confirmed that the second skeleton found was that of Napope, a 16-year-old girl originally from Duck Lake, Saskatchewan.

Armed with this information, Crown prosecutor Terry Hinz petitioned the court to obtain authorization for police to record conversations between Crawford and Bill Corrigan. In early January 1995, Corrigan made the trip from Winnipeg to Saskatoon and called Crawford, letting him know he was in town. The pair met at Corrigan's hotel room on the night of January 9. Corrigan was outfitted with an electronic microphone and transmitter as well as a tape recorder that was affixed to his back. Every word Crawford spoke that night was heard and recorded by investigators.

Corrigan and Crawford got together three times over the next five days, and it took only a matter of hours for Crawford to incriminate himself. Shortly after he arrived at the hotel, Crawford responded to Corrigan's questions about the murders, admitting, "there's only the three I did." He talked about Napope, the woman both he and Corrigan had thought was named Angie, and how any semen left on her body would have decayed before her remains were found. Even though Corrigan prodded him, Crawford denied having anything to do with the murder of Janet Sylvestre, the woman who had accused him of rape.

And then, as the police listened and the tape recorder rolled, John Martin Crawford effectively nailed himself down as Saskatoon's worst serial killer.

"The one I'm worried about is the one with the blanket. I did nothing to her on the blanket. I covered her up. They found the cord, but they wouldn't find my fingerprints. I buried her about this much...others were just on top of the ground," Crawford said.

The RCMP never disclosed that Eva Taysup had been found tied up in an electrical cord, wrapped in a blanket. It was classified as "hold-back evidence," information only the killer would know. By talking about the blanket and the cord, Crawford had in effect just confessed to being her killer.

The pair reconvened twice more over the five days, driving around Saskatoon, drinking and reminiscing about the different hookers they knew. Corrigan used the time to shore up the information Crawford had already told him, as well as prod him a little more about Janet Sylvestre's murder. Crawford, however, did not bite, repeatedly saying he was home the night she died.

On their third night together, the two men picked up a prostitute named Barb. Corrigan took his allotted time with the woman to warn her not to be alone with Crawford.

The police investigation was as solid as it would ever be. Crawford had incriminated himself on tape, and they had Corrigan's testimony, even though they had to buy it. The same week Corrigan and Crawford

were reminiscing, the police finally released the identity of the third victim. The first skeleton found at
Bare Ass Beach belonged to Calinda Waterhen, 22,
a resident of Loon Lake, Saskatchewan.

On Tuesday, January 17, the RCMP again told
reporters that they had few leads in the investigation
into the murders and were desperate for information.

Two days later, eight police officers moved in on
Crawford as he drove down Avenue M South in Saskatoon. One police car cut him off while the rest
swooped in to stop his escape. The strategy proved to
be overly cautious, because Crawford offered no resis-
tance. The only thing he said, upon learning he was
being charged with three counts of first-degree murder, was that he wanted a lawyer.

❧❖❧

According to a 2002 article printed in the Chilliwack Times, Native women make up 2.5 percent of
Canada's population. They are five times more likely
to die a violent death than any other group of women
in the country.

Crawford's 1996 trial on three counts of first-degree
murder garnered little in the way of national press coverage, because the violent death or murder of a woman
of First Nations descent is common, especially in Saskatchewan. In addition, Crawford's trial was getting
underway less than a year after Paul Bernardo was
convicted by an Ontario jury of two counts of first-
degree murder.

The two cases were in stark contrast to one another. Paul Bernardo was an attractive, successful man who had, with his wife Karla Homolka, kidnapped, raped and killed two Ontario school girls. The rapes were videotaped, their bodies dismembered and discarded. The victims were bright, attractive, white teenagers with their whole futures ahead of them. In Saskatoon, Crawford, a heavy-set, unattractive man whose IQ made him as unremarkable as white paint, was charged with three counts of first-degree murder in the sex slayings of three Native women. The women were cast as dregs of Saskatoon's population, women who drank heavily, used drugs and may or may not have been prostitutes. Their killings were as tragic as those that had occurred in Ontario, yet the country chose instead to focus its attention on the monster that was Bernardo.

The local media, of course, lent some coverage to Crawford's trial, which began on May 19, 1996. Presided over by Court of Queen's Bench Justice David Wright, a jury of six men and six women was chosen by Crown prosecutor Terry Hinz and defence counsels Mark Brayford and Hugh Harradence. Victoria Crawford had secured the services of the two lawyers, regarded as two of the best in Saskatchewan, at a hefty retainer.

"Murders are assaults where somebody died. The stakes are a little higher, that's all," Hinz said in his opening remarks.

Tight as the case may have seemed, the Crown knew it would have a tough time securing all three first-degree murder charges. Under the Criminal Code of Canada, a person commits first-degree murder if they deliberately plan and cause the death of another person or if a person is killed during a sexual assault. Hinz knew he had little evidence pointing to the fact Crawford had raped all three women before killing them. He chose, however, to proceed with the charges and see how the trial went.

Brayford and Harradence also had a difficult trial in front of them. Their client was not exactly a poster boy for good citizenship, and the detailed conversations on the tape recorded by Bill Corrigan in January 1995 would be difficult to discount. The lawyers' strategy at the outset was to paint Corrigan as a disreputable character whose motivation for his involvement in the case was purely financial. If they could convince at least one person on the jury that their client was no worse than Corrigan, then they might be able to secure a mistrial.

Brayford had always stated that all persons in Canada are entitled to a vigorous defence, and he was as determined to fight for Crawford as he would have been for any other accused individual. Both he and Harradence took dead aim at the police during the first few days of the trial, peppering investigators with questions about every aspect of their case. Harradence countered successive witnesses who attended the Eva Taysup crime scene about the media presence at the dump site. His theory was that the media had been close enough to hear about the holdback evidence— the blanket and electrical cord—and had published that information. Subsequently, he argued, Crawford might have learned about it through a newspaper story or television report. Despite Harradence's efforts, though, no one could produce evidence that any of the local media had reported the holdback evidence on even a single occasion.

Dr. Ernie Walker, the anthropology professor who had examined the victims' remains, testified about the condition in which they were found. He was unable to determine a cause of death in any of the three cases but described the damage done to Eva Taysup's remains, including the broken jaw, rib and the sawed-off left arm. Despite Brayford's suggestions to the contrary, Walker was emphatic that the arm had been sawed off, not chewed off by animals in the area.

"This is absolutely not from chewing," he said, gesturing to a photo of the amputated stump.

The third day of the trial, from the Crown's perspective, was the most important. Hinz played the Corrigan tapes as well as providing the jury with written transcripts of the conversations. While Constable Al Keller narrated in between the playbacks, the jury listened to Crawford's own voice describing his involvement in the three murders.

"Why did you kill them, John?" Corrigan asked at one point.

"They made me mad," Crawford responded.

Crawford talked about how he had killed Eva Taysup behind a cement factory because she was going to accuse him of rape, even though he had already paid her for her services. He had planned to go back and dis-member her entire corpse, but never got around to it.

He also spoke about how he had intended to return to Shelley Napope's body and knock all of her teeth out to make identifying her remains more difficult. He went on to tell Corrigan that he and Calinda Water-hen had sniffed solvents in the bushes, and claimed: "I hit her over the head."

Through it all, the defence never disputed it was their client's voice on the tape. They had admitted early on that they would not contest the identity of the three victims. They were waiting for Bill Corrigan. On the fourth day of the trial, they finally got their chance.

The Crown opened that day by having Corrigan describe the night Crawford killed Napope and how the trio had been drinking in the woods near Bare Ass Beach when Crawford told Corrigan to get lost. Cor-rigan talked about how Napope had begged him for help while Crawford hauled her into the woods, but he hadn't done anything.

"I saw John with a knife in his hand," Corrigan tes-tified, near tears. "She was lying on the ground, flat on her back. She was bleeding."

It never phased Crawford, said Corrigan.

"I asked him if he realized what he had done. He just kind of laughed. Said not to worry."

In between the Crown's case and the defence cross-examination, however, the case against Crawford suf-fered a minor setback. Hinz was hoping to introduce some "similar fact evidence" into the case—testimony of alleged crimes for which Crawford had not been convicted. Hinz had two stories he wanted put before the jury—those of Louise Alice LeMay and Melanie Fiddler, two women who came forward after Crawford's arrest with accusations of rape and assault. Hinz knew he had little evidence showing that either Waterhen or Taysup were sexually assaulted before they had died. Therefore, he hoped that by putting LeMay and Fiddler's evidence before the jury he could demonstrate what had likely happened before Waterhen and Taysup died.

The defence countered sharply, arguing the extremely prejudicial effect such evidence would have on the case. They cited repeated instances of case law in which it was determined the Crown was required to prove that the probative value of any similar-fact evidence outweighed its prejudicial effect. After adjourning for the weekend, Justice Wright returned to court on Monday and ruled against the Crown's motion. The evidence would not be heard.

With that argument successfully behind him, Brayford went after Corrigan. He made it known, both through Corrigan's testimony and previous police witnesses, that Corrigan was being paid for his help. He itemized Corrigan's criminal record, describing some of the 50 entries to the jury. He implied that Corrigan was untrustworthy because of his reputation as a snitch: he was just looking out for his own best interests.

As aggressive as Brayford was, however, he was obviously trying to climb a steep hill in his attempt to bring down Bill Corrigan. Brayford resurrected the murder of Janet Sylvestre—Crawford's former accuser—and asked Corrigan where he was on the day Sylvestre was last seen. In fact, Brayford had hired a private detective to dig into Corrigan's life and discovered that he had not reported to work in Winnipeg on that day. Although Brayford hammered him with this fact, Corrigan refused to budge, asserting he had not been in Saskatoon that day.

Having exhausted his defence, Brayford concluded his questioning early that Monday afternoon. Hinz then informed the court Corrigan had been the Crown's last witness.

The following day, Brayford rose in court and informed both Wright and the jury that the defence would not call any evidence. John Martin Crawford did not get the chance to explain himself.

Hinz was brief and deliberate in his closing statement, recounting the evidence and doing his best to refute some of the defence's implications about Bill Corrigan. Brayford's closing statement again picked up on Corrigan's character and explained to the jury that Corrigan's role in the investigation raised the specter of reasonable doubt in the case.

"The amount of talking that John Crawford does on the tape is minute. William Corrigan talks all the time. The reason he talks all the time is that he doesn't want my client to get a word in edgewise."

The next day, Wright began issuing his charge to the jury. But before Wright started, Hinz rose and informed the court he was withdrawing the first-degree murder charges in the deaths of Waterhen and Taysup, replacing them with charges of second-degree murder. Wright spent two hours detailing some of the evidence the jury had heard, explaining points of law and outlining the options open to them under the Criminal Code of Canada. In all three cases, said Wright, the jury could consider convictions of manslaughter. He warned them against buying into Brayford's speculation that Bill Corrigan had killed Janet Sylvestre but also cautioned them against putting too much stock in Corrigan's evidence.

"It is unsafe to rely on the evidence of a person like Corrigan in isolation," said Wright.

The jury was excused at noon and began their deliberations shortly after lunch.

At 10:20 PM that night, the court sheriff announced the jury had reached a verdict. Once the court was reassembled, the jury filed in and the foreman answered the questions of the clerk of the court. John Martin Crawford was found guilty of one count of first-degree murder and two counts of second-degree murder.

Under the Criminal Code of Canada, convictions of both first- and second-degree murder carry mandatory life sentences; the only difference is parole eligibility. In the case of first-degree murder, an offender must serve 25 years before being eligible. In the case of second-degree murder, the judge can impose a minimum of 10 years to a maximum of 25 years before an offender is eligible.

Justice Wrigh required little time to make his decision. The next morning, having heard sentencing submissions from both sides the night before, he issued his judgment, barely able to contain his disgust for Crawford.

"[Crawford] seemed determined to destroy every vestige of their humanity. He left three of them naked and lying on the ground. There is a kind of ferocity in these actions that reminds me of a wild animal, a predator," said Wright.

Subsequently, Wright ordered that Crawford serve three concurrent life sentences with no eligibility for parole in each instance for the full 25 years. He also took the unusual step of endorsing the file for the National Parole Board, meaning that his remarks would be available to the board when Crawford did come up for parole.

The press accorded Crawford's conviction some coverage, but he soon fell from the public eye. So too did his victims, as few of their relatives attended the trial.

On January 21, 1999, Crawford appeared before the Saskatchewan Court of Appeal with a new lawyer hired by his mother. Bob Hrycan argued the conviction should be overturned because Crawford had been represented by ineffective counsel. In an affidavit filed with the court, Crawford confessed to his crimes for the first time ever. He described consuming Ritalin, Talwin, marijuana, Valium and several beer on the day he met Eva Taysup. He choked her to death when she said she would cry rape if he didn't pay her more money. He choked Calinda Waterhen after she demanded $100 for her company instead of the $45 Crawford gave her.

Furthermore, Crawford claimed that Bill Corrigan had killed Shelley Napope, not him. He had, however, stabbed her 18 more times after Corrigan allegedly cut her throat, just to make sure she was dead.

The three-judge panel took less than 15 minutes to reach their decision. Crawford's appeal was denied.

One year later, the Supreme Court of Canada dismissed an appeal by Crawford's attorney without explanation.

John Martin Crawford is currently serving three con-current life sentences at the Regional Psychiatric Centre in Saskatoon. He will be eligible for full parole in 2020.

He has not been charged in the death of Janet Sylvestre.

CHAPTER SEVEN

Robert William Pickton
(1949–)

November 2001

NO MATTER HOW FAST SHE RAN, SHE COULDN'T ESCAPE THE screaming.

Desperate, frightened and high, the woman crashed through the night with all the subtlety of a dump truck, stumbling on uneven ground and sobbing as her legs churned the earth. Over the sounds of her friend's screams, all the woman could hear were her own frantic gasps.

She spied a row of hedges not far away and slipped behind them, collapsing to the earth and trying to calm down. Her heart was racing, partly from the adrenaline coursing through her veins and partly from the crack she had smoked earlier. She clenched her eyes shut, trying not to cry as she listened to her friend scream into the night.

The night had started off in a promising way—well, as promising as any night in Low Track could be. She had hit the streets before midnight, strolling up and down her beat, trying to entice would-be suitors to her corner. It had been a slow night for the most part, just a few johns willing to part with their cash for a quickie in the back of their cars. It was looking like it was going to be a late night, and then he showed up.

The second she saw him, the woman knew her fortune had changed. He wasn't much to look at, but she had been with him once before and he'd paid her $100 for her time, more than most tricks. He'd also had good crack, and he hadn't charged her for it.

He had lied the last time. He got her into the car by saying he just wanted someone to party with. They'd gone back to his home—where it was she wasn't sure—and smoked a few rocks. Sure enough, however, he changed his mind and decided he wanted his money's worth. It wasn't worth putting up a fight, she decided. After all, he'd paid her, she had no idea where she was and she was really too high to care.

So when he'd pulled up tonight and asked her if she wanted to party again, she'd said yes and hopped in. He then told her he wanted to pick up another girl to party with. She picked one of her friends who she'd gone on "double dates" with in the past.

It had all started out so wonderfully for a work night, heading back to his trailer to have a good time. They knocked back a few drinks, and then he disappeared and came back with a few more rocks of crack and told them to enjoy themselves. Crack was her thing, it was what she loved, it was why she was selling herself out on the street to strangers. Her first hit so long ago had been so blissful, so pure. She'd never felt anything like it before and she never did again. Granted, getting high was better than staying straight, but for all the crack she smoked, it never felt like that first time.

So when the john's mood changed, when he suddenly started yelling and raving, it had taken her a moment to clue into what was going on. One minute they were partying and having fun, and the next he was saying that they were going to rob him. She thought he was just having a bad trip, but he wouldn't let it go. He kept yelling and screaming, and it suddenly started to dawn on her that she had no idea where she was and no idea how to get back to Low Track.

"I could kill you," he suddenly yelled. "I could kill you and I'd get away with it because nobody cares about you. You're just a couple of whores."

This was definitely getting out of hand. She'd talked with a few of the girls after the first time she'd gone with him and got mixed reviews. Some liked him because of all the drugs he had, but some said he was a bad date with a mean streak. That didn't matter now. What did matter was that he was tripping out right in front of them, and no one knew where they were.

It happened so fast she almost didn't see it. His hand flashed down to a side table where she noticed only then that two knives were on display. He grabbed one of the knives and suddenly lunged at her friend. That was all it took. Panicked and hysterical, she'd bolted from her chair and run out the door.

Her breathing was softer now, but the world still spun a bit as her high lingered. She knew she'd broken the golden rule: never leave another girl behind. But what else could she do? If she'd stayed, what would she have done?

Suddenly the screaming tapered off and then stopped altogether, and she knew her friend was not okay, but there was nothing she could do. It was late, she was high and she didn't have her purse or any money with her. She didn't even know how she was going to get home.

Eventually she picked herself up out of the hedge and made her way to a nearby road, all the while keeping an eye out for her friend. She walked against traffic, holding her thumb out until someone finally stopped and picked her up. Within a couple of hours, she was back in Low Track.

She stumbled into her room at the flophouse and dug another rock of crack out of her stash, smoking it as fast as the pipe would allow. She prayed as she inhaled, wishing for the drugs to take away the memory of what she'd been through, but it was no use. She remembered everything.

The next morning she went looking for her friend but never found her. No one had seen the other woman, and by the end of the day she knew that something had gone horribly wrong. But who was she going to tell?

"You're just a couple of whores," he'd said, and he was right.

Who was going to care?

Although some may say it sparkles like a jewel on the West Coast, the city of Vancouver is not without its eyesores. One of them is Low Track.

Low Track is what they call the city's Downtown Eastside. Some call it the Tenderloin District. It is a 10-block sewer of human squalor in the area around Main and Hastings (which most inhabitants refer to simply as "Pain and Wastings"). Rife with gang activity, prostitution and drugs, its streets are dotted with pawnshops, rundown bars, fleabag motels and flophouses. At night, the working girls take over, flaunting their bodies streetside for as little as $20 or as much as it will take to buy their next fix. Those who cannot make the money will steal it, raiding people's homes in lightning-fast break and enters and stealing anything of value in sight.

Millions came to Vancouver in 1986 when the city was awarded the Expo, hoping to cash in on the economic boom that was sure to follow. When the geodesic dome and monorail were packed up, however, there was little left for the unskilled. The drug trade flourished, centred around the Downtown Eastside. While other Canadian provinces began cutting welfare payments, BC began bolstering its social programs, making the province and its largest city an attractive beacon to adventure seekers and runaways. Most that did come, however, found their bliss only in a glass pipe or a dirty syringe.

At first, heroin was the drug of choice in Low Track, but addicts soon learned they could shoot cocaine 15 to 20 times a day for the cost of a few hits of smack. Women continued to prostitute themselves by night and then spent their days shooting up in alleys and doorways. They were less concerned about things like hygiene and health, about HIV and AIDS, and more focused on getting their next fix. The last thing anyone wanted to worry about when they were going to get high was whether or not their needle was clean. It was just as easy to borrow someone else's.

The effect led to the first-ever public health emergency in BC's history in Confederation as the rate of HIV infection among the 6000 to 10,000 junkies in Low Track exploded. Each year, the number of new HIV cases climbed 27 percent through the 1990s. By 2000, Vancouver had the highest rate of HIV infection in all of North America.

The government did its best to tackle the problem. In 1994, they implemented a needle-exchange program, handing out free sterile syringes for every used one turned in. But the program didn't help. It was just as easy to keep using the needles you already had instead of going to the hassle of trading them in. Although the government gave out 2.5 million free syringes each year, the program did little to stem the ballooning infection rate. By 1998 the city recorded one death by overdose per day.

The easiest way for women to pay for drugs, especially when they don't care about anything else, is to become a prostitute. In Vancouver's Downtown East-side, it is the easiest job to find. There are as many men willing to pimp women as there are men willing to pay for their services, and at the end of a trick, the women have some cash in hand to buy drugs.

There are prostitutes in Vancouver as young as 11 years old, pimped out in special, secure trick pads. They are runaways and adventure seekers from outside the city who come to Vancouver to try to find some small sliver of life worthy of holding on to. Eighty percent of Vancouver's sex-trade workers were born and raised outside the city. Seventy-three percent of area prostitutes began working when they were still technically children.

Those numbers, however, are difficult to confirm because of the transitory nature of the lifestyle. A prostitute does not have to give out her social insurance number to begin selling her body. Many don't have leases, bank accounts or phones. They may move thousands of kilometres away without telling anyone. A few women may find the gut-wrenching inner strength necessary to lift themselves up out of "the life," get clean and find a job worthy of them. Most, however, are condemned to a life of disease, violence and death. Many die from poor health or drug over-doses, or at the hands of a violent pimp or john, and, too often, no one comes to claim the body. They are simply claimed by the province and buried in a "municipal plot," the 21st century's equivalent of a pauper's grave.

So when prostitutes began disappearing from the Downtown Eastside in the early 1980s, no one paid much attention, least of all the Vancouver police. As it was, friends and family often waited months or years before reporting a girl missing. Although Rebecca Guno was first reported missing on June 25, 1983, only three days after she was last seen, it took three years before anyone bothered to report 43-year-old Sherry Rail's disappearance in 1987. Elaine Auerbach, 33, told her friends she was moving to Seattle in March 1986 but never arrived, and though her case was reported to police in April, no one thought much of it. Teresa Williams, 26, was reported missing in March 1989, almost a year after she had last been seen. No one bothered reporting the disappearance of Ingrid Soet, 40, until October 1990, 14 months after anyone remembered her last-known whereabouts. In June 1992, friends reported that Kathleen Wattley, 39, hadn't been seen for a while.

Had it stopped there, no one might have even noticed what was actually going on in Low Track, and for a while it seemed as if that might very well be the case. Between 1992 and 1995, there were no reports of women missing from the Downtown Eastside. In February 1996, however, Cathy Gonzales, 47, was reported missing, 11 months after vanishing from sight. Catherine Knight, 32, disappeared in April 1995 and wasn't reported missing until November of that year. No one had seen Dorothy Spence, a 36-year-old woman of First Nations descent, since August 1995 when her friends reported her missing at the end of

October. Between December 1995 and 1996, Diana Melnick, Tanya Holyk and Olivia Williams all vanished from Low Track.

Frightening as the trend was, the disappearances continued to increase. Seven Low Track prostitutes disappeared in 1997. August was the most deadly month—Marnie Frey, 25, Helen Hallmark, 32, and Jacqueline Murdock, 28, all vanished. By the end of 1997, friends or family reported to police a total of 19 sex-trade workers missing from the Downtown Eastside, but there was still no action forthcoming.

Both Kerry Koski and Jacqueline McDonnell vanished in January 1998. One month later, Inga Hall, 46, disappeared. On April 14, 1998, friends reported Sarah Jane Devries, 29, missing, the same day they had last seen her. Investigators found a diary among her belongings that detailed her losing battle with drug addiction.

"I think my hate is going to be my destination or my executioner," she wrote.

By the time Sheila Egan, a 20-year-old who began working as a prostitute at the age of 15, was reported missing on August 5, 1998, some people were finally starting to take notice. First and foremost, it was the women themselves who knew something was happening. Counterintuitive as it may seem, the world of prostitution is often a close-knit one, with women working in groups and looking out for one another. Information and rumour spills through the Downtown Eastside faster than any telephone line. Girls were disappearing, they knew, and weren't coming back. They weren't turning up in the morgue, and no one believed for a second that every single one of the 24 women who had gone missing since 1983 had been able to pull herself out of the life.

The girls began passing their information on to social workers from the aid agencies that tried to help them break free from drugs and prostitution. In September 1998, a group who worked with Aboriginal women officially presented the Vancouver Police with a list of women from the Downtown Eastside who they believed had been murdered.

The length of the list quickly grabbed the department's attention, and officers began to run the names down. Some had died from overdoses. A few others had moved away from Vancouver, with fewer still who had managed to rebuild their lives.

When police combined their list with a list of all the missing persons reports originating from Low Track, they realized there might be a larger problem in their midst than originally expected. By now, the media had begun to ask about the women, keyed onto the issue by other sources familiar with what was going on. In an attempt to show the public that the police were taking the issue seriously, the department announced the formation of the Joint Missing Women's Task Force.

Their task, however, was not an easy one. Disappearances, at first glance, were not criminal in nature and consequently were difficult to track. There were no bodies, no crime scenes, no witnesses and no evidence. Disappearances could not be logged in the RCMP's Violent Crime Linkage System because the nationwide database did not accept missing persons reports without either a body or evidence of foul play. Pimps and streetwalkers were reluctant to assist the officers with their investigation, fearing retribution or arrest. Family members often hadn't seen their daughters or sisters for years before their disappearance and therefore could provide little information.

From the public's perspective, another problem critically afflicted the task force's investigation: malaise. The women they were chasing were drug addicts and prostitutes, and though any self-respecting police officer will maintain that any person, regardless of the way he or she lived, is still someone's daughter or son, that attitude seemed lacking dating back to the first disappearances in the 1980s. Follow-ups of initial missing persons reports were cursory and skeptical, given the propensity for streetwalkers to either overdose or simply move away.

Yet the Vancouver Police Department and the surrounding RCMP detachments had had an object lesson in such thinking only a decade before prostitutes began disappearing with any regularity. Between 1980 and 1981, Clifford Olson had kidnapped, sexually assaulted and murdered as many as 13 teenagers, boys and girls. In several of the disappearances, the police had less than vigorously pursued missing persons reports of teens with a history of running away or troublemaking. That oversight cost the lives of several more victims.

It was only by forming a special task force in the summer of 1981 that the RCMP had finally realized the scope of the problem and been able to arrest Olson.

Publicly, the Joint Missing Women's Task Force stated only that it was investigating the disappearances of a list of women in the Vancouver area, which later grew to include all of BC. Shortly after the task force's formation, the list had 40 names dating back to 1971. By 2001, the list included 54 names that were being pursued and investigated by as many as 85 RCMP and Vancouver police officers.

The task force, however, refused to state publicly that they were pursuing a serial killer or killers, even though the rumour was circulating through the city. At least one officer had already produced some work that lent credence to the idea: in May 1999, Inspector Kim Rossmo reported to his superiors that he had completed a geographic profile of the disappearances. "Geoprofiling" is a mathematical technique that links related offences by location and tries to predict a serial offender's most likely place of work and the characteristics of the particular neighbourhood. Rossmo's profile showed a cluster of disappearances had taken place in the city's Downtown Eastside. The profile was the first substantial development that pointed to a serial killer preying on Low Track prostitutes.

The task force brass didn't buy the idea that a serial killer might be at work. They stated to the public their belief that the women had simply moved onto greener pastures. Rossmo resigned shortly after he received a punitive demotion.

While the task force rejected the idea of a serial killer on the prowl when asked by the media, the officers working the case did their best to rule out the possibility. Investigators scoured coroners' reports, burial records, and police files from detachments throughout Canada and the U.S., trying to scratch as many names as possible from their list. They called and visited drug rehabilitation centres, psychiatric wards, hospitals and palliative care units for patients living with AIDS. Their efforts yielded some success. Patricia Perkins, who had disappeared in 1981, called the task force in December 1999 to inform them she was very much alive and now drug free. Investigators found Rose Ann Jenson after searching through a national health care database. Somber officers also learned that Linda Jean Coombes had died of a heroin overdose, and that Karen Anne Smith had died in Edmonton of complications from hepatitis C.

Even as the investigation unfolded, the disappearances continued. Julie Young vanished in October 1998 but wasn't reported missing until the following June. Angela Jardine, a 28-year-old prostitute with the mental acuity of a 10-year-old, vanished in November. One month later, Michelle Gurney, 30, disappeared. Two days after Christmas, Marcella Creison, 20, was released from jail and was supposed to return home to her boyfriend and mother. She never arrived.

The task force decided the best tactic would be to start interviewing potential suspects: those who were already known to police for similar crimes. They first looked at a man named Michael Leopold, 36, who had recently been arrested for attacking a prostitute. According to witnesses, Leopold had tried to shove a rubber ball down the woman's throat before he was scared off by some people in the area. Leopold admitted during questioning that though he had often fantasized about being violent towards women, the attack was his first attempt to bring his fantasies to life. Lacking any evidence to the contrary, the police discarded him as a suspect. He was later sentenced to 14 years in jail for the attack.

Barry Thomas, 43, arrested once in 1990 for pimping out a 14-year-old girl, was another potential suspect. In April 2000, he was arrested for allegedly attacking several Vancouver prostitutes. The charges against him warranted a closer look: sexual assault, kidnapping, assault, robbery, unlawful confinement and administering a noxious substance. None of his victims, however, were the women reported missing from the Downtown Eastside.

In some instances, the police found themselves chasing phantom suspects. In August 2001, a 38-year-old woman reported to police that she had been attacked and raped by a man. During the assault, the man claimed he was responsible for assaulting and killing several women from Low Track. The woman had escaped the man's vehicle by jumping out of it while it was still moving. The victim couldn't provide a description, and efforts to find the attacker yielded no results.

The public was certainly helpful, calling in with tips about suspects. All together, the police had tracked down as many as 600 people at any given time as suspects in the missing women case. In 1998, a 37-year-old man added another name to their list: Bill Hiscox contacted the police and said that he thought his boss might be involved in the disappearances. Hiscox worked for a salvage company in Surrey that was owned by Robert William Pickton and his brother, David.

Hiscox told police he often picked up his paycheques from the Picktons' pig farm located 35 kilometres outside Vancouver in Port Coquitlam, a large property he described as "creepy." In addition, he told police that the Picktons often hosted large parties that featured roasted pigs, ducks, plenty of booze and at least one, if not more, prostitute who worked out of the Downtown Eastside. Hiscox said he knew Robert, known to his friends as Willie, often used the services of girls from Low Track. Hiscox also claimed he had seen evidence on the property that further bolstered his suspicions.

Hiscox also told police that Pickton had only one year previously been charged with attempted murder. Although the details of the arrest warrant in the 1997 case have since been subject to a publication ban, it is known that he was charged with the offence in March 1997. Pickton put up $2000 bail after being arrested. The charges were later stayed by the Crown in 1998.

The task force decided to dig deeper into Pickton's history. Robert was born in 1949 to Helen and Leonard Pickton. He was the second of two sons who also grew up with their sister Linda. In 1963 Leonard and Helen purchased 40 acres of swampland outside Vancouver for $18,000 and moved the family and their farmhouse to the site. They raised pigs while bringing up the trio. Dave and Robert were raised on the farm. Linda was sent into the city to a boarding school.

Leonard died in 1978, and Helen succumbed to cancer a year later. All three children eventually inherited the estate, the worth of which had skyrocketed as Vancouver continued to grow. A 1994 assessment pegged the farmland's value at approximately $7 million. The Pickton children cashed in on their growing fortunes, selling a part of their farm to a developer for $1.7 million to build townhouses. The city of Port Coquitlam also bought a parcel for $1.2 million to build a park, while the school district bought a $2.3 million chunk in 1995 and built an elementary school.

The Pickton brothers, however, had not escaped life without notice. In 1992, Dave was convicted of sexual assault after a woman claimed she had been attacked in his trailer. Dave was fined $1000 and sentenced to 30 days probation.

The brothers were sued three times for three different car accidents but later settled out of court. In the meantime, the brothers set up the Piggy Palace Good

Times Society, a registered charity that claimed their mandate was to organize social functions for other service groups. According to witnesses, it was said that mayors, city councillors and business people often attended functions at the palace, which was an old banquet hall located on a second property owned by the Picktons. Some neighbours claimed the brothers collected toys for poor children and raised money for charity. Other neighbours remembered loud, raging parties that got so loud and clamorous the city eventually slapped the brothers with an order forbidding any more parties on the property. It was those same parties, said Hiscox, that often turned into drunken binge sessions featuring prostitutes from Low Track.

Subsequent to Hiscox's information, the police visited the pig farm, searching the property as many as three times. Apparently they came up empty-handed because Pickton was later downgraded from a suspect to a "person of interest" in the investigation.

The disappearances, however, did not end. In 1998, Ruby Hardy, 37, vanished, not reported missing until 2002. Wendy Crawford, Jennifer Furminger and Georgina Papin all disappeared in 1999, along with Brenda Wolfe, 32, and Tiffany Drew, 27. Dawn Crey, 42, and Debra Jones, 43, were reported missing in December 2000. Between February and November 2001, eight more women disappeared from the Downtown Eastside: Patricia Johnson, Yvonne Boen, Heather Bottomley, Heather Chinnock, Angela Jonesbury, Sereena Abotsway, Diane Rock and Mona Wilson.

If there was a serial killer at work, he was starting to escalate, killing at a frenzied rate and growing increasingly bold in the frequency with which he scouted out his victims. Growing more concerned with each passing day, the task force searched further afield for potential suspects. The police investigated reports that Gary Leon Ridgeway had visited the city during his 19-year spree as the Green River Killer in Oregon that culminated in the deaths of 48 women. He might have visited the city, but the task force could not tie him to any of the disappearances.

The task force also looked at Ronald Richard McCauley, an offender twice convicted of rape, once in 1982 and again in 1994. The bodies of four Low Track workers had been found between Mission and Agassiz, which was centred roughly around where McCauley lived. The more the task force looked, the better they liked McCauley. In July 1997, the police investigated him for the disappearances of Catherine Gonzales, Catherine Knight and Dorothy Spence, three of the women on their list.

All together, the police now had the names of 144 prostitutes who had disappeared from across the province. The RCMP joined the task force in 2001 but produced little in the way of results in their first year on the job. Investigators began throwing other theories around, supposing the killer was a long-haul trucker who disposed of the bodies across North America or that the prostitutes were being lured onto ships and their bodies discarded at sea. Victims groups and families were clamouring for answers, yet the police didn't seem to have any to give. The task force lent the appearance to the public that someone was doing something about the disappearances, but the unit had no results to point to.

On February 7, 2002, the entire investigation changed. On that day, a spokesperson for the Joint Missing Women's Task Force issued a statement to the press saying authorities had descended on a pig farm and adjacent property and executed a search warrant. Police and forensic experts were at the farm looking for evidence related to the disappearance of several prostitutes from Vancouver's Downtown Eastside.

The owner of the farm was Robert William Pickton, the same man the task force had first been warned about almost four years previously.

The task force went on to state that Pickton had been arrested on illegal firearms charges earlier in the week and had since been freed on bail. His whereabouts, the police stated, were not a matter of concern.

The press flocked to the farmhouse, watching while police search teams and forensic technicians paroled the property and its few ramshackle buildings. A sign on a fence on the farm warned all visitors "this property is protected by a pit bull with AIDS." Strewn about the land were piles of dirt and cement along with old cars. Cadaver dogs scoured the grounds while the police erected a fence around their work area to keep away the prying eyes of the public and the media.

The obvious conclusion, left hanging in the air by the task force, crystallized on February 22 when Pickton was re-arrested by police and charged with two counts of first-degree murder in the disappearances of Sereena Abotsway and Mona Wilson.

Finally unleashed, the press began filing whatever it could discern from the investigation. The details of Pickton's previous charge of attempted murder were reported before a judge could ban publication of the details of the warrant. Lurid stories of what exactly the police found in their initial search of the property dominated the news south of the border, where the U.S. media was not beholden to Canadian law. The task force stated the evidence they found in their initial searches was "substantial." The press reported that human remains had been found in a freezer.

The report illuminated a fact that the police grudgingly acknowledged: they were not looking for intact bodies. The police were looking first and foremost for remains, either large or microscopic. In a meeting with the families of several victims, one coroner reportedly described the crime scene as "a massacre."

The bulk of the search focused on retrieving DNA or belongings of the women on their list. In March 2002, the police met with the families of many of the victims and asked them for details about clothing or jewellery that might help speed up the investigation.

The focus of the search became increasingly clear. As many as 104 forensic anthropologists as well as several university students were working the site, using dump trucks and a conveyor belt to sift through tons of dirt and gravel for human remains, such as bone chips or teeth. Eventually, the search expanded to the second Pickton property located 65 kilometres from Vancouver, home of the infamous party palace. The search team included eight divers.

While the searches continued, the charges against Pickton began to mount. In April, the pig farmer was charged with the murders of Jacqueline McDonnell, Heather Bottomley, Diane Rock and Angela Jones-bury. On May 22, he was charged with first-degree murder in the death of Brenda Wolfe. In October, the police charged him with the murders of Heather Chinnock, Tanya Holyk, Sherry Irving and Inga Hall.

Pickton's neighbours couldn't believe what the police and the press were telling them. Pickton was remembered as a quiet man who never drank or smoked, who just worked on his farm slaughtering pigs privately, then driving their unusable remains to a rendering plant. He and Dave dabbled in demoli-tions and sold gravel and dirt from their farm. Pickton liked to ride motorcycles and allegedly liked to spend time with members of known biker gangs. He was "kind of slow, but hard working and clean living," said one woman.

"I would trust Robert with my life," said Della Grant, 63, a neighbour of the Picktons.

Others, however, were willing to take advantage of Pickton's precarious legal situation. In November 2002, People for the Ethical Treatment of Animals

(PETA) launched an advertising campaign that likened the slaughter of animals for meat to the murders of the women from the Downtown Eastside. The public howled in protest, with one newspaper even going so far as to refuse to run the ads. PETA eventually withdrew the campaign in its entirety. Pickton, however, was not beyond making a little press of his own. His family began protesting his housing conditions at the North Fraser Correctional Centre, claiming he had not been allowed outside for five months. He made his court appearances by a secure video link between the prison and the courthouse. Corrections authorities admitted they were keeping Pickton in segregation, but more for his own safety than out of any form of perceived punishment or injustice. Several relatives of Pickton's alleged victims, they said, were also currently incarcerated at the North Fraser, and the possibility for violence was high.

By October 2002, police had laid 15 charges of first-degree murder against Pickton. By then, the investigation had cost taxpayers $20 million. The DNA of 30 women had been found on the farm, 27 of whom were women on the task force's list of the missing. The investigation was now officially the largest murder case in Canadian law enforcement history.

Peter Ritchie knew that. The BC defence lawyer was representing Pickton in his legal proceedings, and Ritchie was determined to give his client the best possible defence. In October 2002, Ritchie publicly stated he would quit the case if the Crown did not provide some sort of funding arrangement for the case. It was,

he argued, an unusual case with a demanding work-
load. Investigators had already logged 10,000 pieces
of evidence at the two properties. In August 2005, it
was revealed that the province had put a $10 million
mortgage on Pickton's farm to help pay for his defence
team, which now numbered seven members.

By the time Ritchie's funding arrangements had
been sorted out, however, he had a new problem to
contend with. Pickton's preliminary hearing on all
15 counts was scheduled to begin in January 2003.
Under the Criminal Code of Canada, a preliminary
hearing, a pretrial inquiry used to determine whether
or not there is sufficient evidence to justify a criminal
charge, is subject to a publication ban. Although the
Canadian media were as a rule good about observing
the publication ban, their U.S. counterparts were not.
Lured north of the border by the grisly details already
coming out of the investigation, the U.S. media were
paroling Vancouver and waiting in line for a seat at
the preliminary hearing.

The problem had first come to light in 1995 during
the Paul Bernardo trial when members of the U.S.
media began publishing both print and online versions
of the trial for Karla Homolka that was supposed to be
banned from public consumption. The Internet was
also a problem: anyone who attended the trial could
post anything they wanted on the Internet, which
would consequently be accessible to anyone with
a computer and a modem. In Ritchie's view, this would
compromise his client's right to a fair trial. He subsequently asked Provincial Court Judge David Stone,

who was hearing the preliminary case, not just to impose a publication ban, but to close the courtroom to both the media and the public at large. The judge refused the request but warned the media that anyone caught violating the ban could be barred from the courtroom for the duration of the proceedings.

The preliminary hearing hadn't even begun when, in December 2002, several U.S. media outlets reported details of the case covered by the publication ban. The material was available on the World Wide Web to anyone who wanted to read it. Several editions of an American newspaper that printed the story were also available for sale in Vancouver.

The furor over the story, however, did not disrupt the proceedings, and the hearing began in January 2003. Even while the hearings continued, the police continued to find more evidence implicating Pickton in the disappearances. The hearing had not even wrapped up when the Crown began musing that it could lay more charges against Pickton. The results of the "prelim" were predictable. On July 23, 2003, Stone ordered Pickton to stand trial on 15 counts of first-degree murder.

Four months later, the police wrapped up their search of the pig farm after almost 18 months of searching. Investigators took 150,000 swabs for DNA from the site and identified the remains of 31 total women. Unfortunately, finding a woman's DNA did not automatically mean a charge of first-degree murder was forthcoming. Several families were informed that while their relatives' DNA put them at the farm at some point, it was not enough to substantiate a charge.

With rumours of more charges forthcoming, the public sat back and waited for a trial date to be set, a date that kept being moved further and further back. The province's health officer, Dr. Perry Kendall, meanwhile, shocked the public back into the case in March 2004 when he announced at a news conference that the province could not guarantee that human remains had not been mixed into the pork products that were sold out of the Pickton farm. Fortunately for the Canadian public at large, the Picktons only gave their products to close friends or neighbours. Those people were urged to return any unconsumed portions to the police for testing. Kendall even went so far as to reassure anyone who had eaten any of the product from the Pickton farm that if the meat had been thoroughly cooked, there was likely no health risk from having consumed it.

The case against Pickton was delayed again in May 2005 when the Crown announced they were laying 12 new charges of first-degree murder against Pickton, bringing the total number of counts to 27. A federal court judge was selected to preside over the trial, but Mr. Justice Geoffrey Barrow was later forced to withdraw from the case due to scheduling concerns. In June 2005, the province appointed Mr. Justice James Williams, a 12-year veteran of the BC Supreme Court to hear the case. Defence counsel Ritchie got to work, asking Williams to ban anyone attending any of Pickton's pretrial hearings from discussing anything they heard with any other member of the public, with the exception of journalists and their editors. Predictably, Williams denied the request.

In January 2006, the Pickton trial opened with a voir dire, a hearing held during a trial so that a judge can evaluate whether or not evidence is admissible at trial. All voir dires are subject to a publication ban on their contents, but Williams did cut Ritchie one break: he said in March 2006 that one charge of first-degree murder in the case of a woman known only as Jane Doe would be thrown out for lack of evidence.

As of the writing of this book, Robert William Pickton's voir dire continues. His trial proper has been scheduled to begin in January 2007 with jury selection, a process that could draw on as many as 3500 members of the public in order to find a 12-person jury acceptable to both the Crown and the defence.

On August 9, 2006, Mr. Justice James Williams ruled that trying Pickton on all 26 counts of murder would pose an unreasonable hardship on a jury, given that the defence had speculated such a trial could last as long as two years. Williams instead ordered Pickton to stand trial on six counts of murder in the deaths of Sereena Abotsway, Marnie Frey, Andrea Jonesbury, Georgina Papin, Mona Wilson and Brenda Wolfe. The Crown will be able to try Pickton on the remaining 20 counts at a later date. Pickton is still being held at the North Fraser Correctional Centre. His guilt has not yet been proven in a court of law.

CHAPTER EIGHT

Project KARE
(2003–)

THE WORLD'S FIRST IMAGE OF THOMAS GEORGE SVELKA WAS a peculiar one.

When Svelka, under police escort, arrived at the courthouse in Fort Saskatchewan for his first court appearance, the media were waiting. TV camera crews and newspaper photographers clustered around, jostling to get their first shot of the man arrested only the previous day.

As he was led into the courthouse, Svelka looked out at the sea of cameras capturing his every move and, raising his handcuffed hands, waved.

A peculiar grin spread across his face. He dropped his hands, then brought a single finger up to his lips, as if urging the entire world that was watching to be quiet.

It wasn't just Svelka's behaviour that guaranteed his notoriety in the capital region. The 38-year-old mechanic stood as a milestone for a joint police task force that was investigating the disappearances and murders of several women in Alberta. Since Project KARE in 2004 started investigating the disappearances of women who had lived high-risk lifestyles, investigators had not yet made a single arrest.

Svelka was their first, arrested on May 8, 2006. Shortly after he was taken into custody, Svelka was charged with second-degree murder in the death of Theresa Merrie Innes, a 36-year-old street worker from Edmonton. He was also charged with interfering with a dead body. According to the RCMP, they found Innes' remains packed in a hockey bag at the home of Svelka's sister.

In the arrest warrant, the RCMP alleged that Innes had been murdered in High Level sometime between May 4 and May 8, 2006. On the day Svelka was arrested, the police searched two different rooms at the Family Motel in High Level. They also seized a red truck that had been parked at the High Level tire company where Svelka worked as a mechanic.

Publicly, the RCMP stated Svelka was only under arrest for the murder of Theresa Innes. The media, however, were starting to wonder. Since 1997, the bodies of 12 women, most of whom were associated with Edmonton's sex-trade industry, had turned up in fields in and around the city. To date, Svelka is the only man arrested in the murder of any sex-trade workers from the capital region. That, says Mike Sekela, team commander of Project KARE, warrants some attention.

"At this moment we have a person in custody in relation to Innes only," said Inspector Sekela. "We have not totally excluded nor included him in any other KARE-mandated cases at this time."

Edmonton's sex-trade industry is mostly found on the streets wrapping around the downtown core. East of 97 Street, transgendered prostitutes try to sell themselves to the curious. Farther south, young men try to attract the attention of other men.

However, on 118 Avenue, farther north, is where the bulk of the city's sex-trade industry thrives. In an area of rundown stores, pawnshops and liquor stores, women dressed in revealing clothes pack the sidewalks along the avenue, waving at cars. Every morning after a weekend night, the residential yards in the area are littered with garbage from convenience stores, used condoms and the occasional syringe. A large percentage of the women working the streets are of First Nations descent, and most of them have some sort of substance abuse problem. Many of them have had a child at one time or another, and their lives are now filled with violence and despair.

And someone, or more than one person, in the capital region is preying on them.

In 1983, the skeletal remains of a young woman, Gail Cardinal, a 21-year-old sex worker, were found in a farm field 10 kilometres south of Fort Saskatchewan. No cause of death was determined, and no one has ever been arrested in her death. The police suspected foul play was involved, and the media now view Cardinal's death as the beginning of a string of murders that highlights the growing vulnerability of Edmonton's sex-trade workers.

In 1986 the body of 21-year-old Melodie Joy Riegel was found on a hotel-room bed in Edmonton. The young prostitute was last seen with a "client."

Two years later, the body of 20-year-old Georgette Flint was found in Elk Island National Park, approximately 50 kilometres east of Edmonton. No cause of death was determined. The discovery of her body was followed in 1989 by that of Bernadette Ahenakew, a 22-year-old mother of three, whose body was found in a ditch alongside a rural road near Sherwood Park.

In October 1990, the police found the body of Mavis Mason, 29, on a rural road west of Edmonton. She had been stabbed to death. Two months later, the strangled body of Lorraine Wray, a 46-year-old masseuse, was discovered in the bathroom of her studio in the city's west end.

The partially decomposed body of Elaine Ross, 25, was found under a bed in a motel room on the city's west end in February 1993. Three years later, Joanne Ghostkeeper, 24, was strangled to death in her east-side apartment.

As the years passed, the body count increased, and a geographic pattern began to emerge. In 1997, the bodies of Joyce Hewitt, Jessica Cardinal and Cara King were all found. All three women had lived high-risk lifestyles. Of the three, King and Hewitt were found in fields in and around Sherwood Park, an Edmonton satellite community policed by the Strathcona County RCMP. Although Kelly Dawn Reilly, 24, was found in a field northwest of the city, and Edna Bernard's burned remains were found in a field near Leduc, the bodies of Monique Pitre, 30, and Melissa Munch, 20, were found four days apart in fields in the Strathcona County area, 5 kilometres away from each other.

The discovery of the bodies of murdered sex-trade workers continued to drift south and east of Edmonton as the death toll continued to climb. A skull belonging to Debbie Lake, 29, was found at Miquelon Lake Provincial Park, 70 kilometres southeast of Edmonton, in April 2003. Three months later, the body of Katie Sylvia Ballantyne, a known sex-trade worker, turned up in a field 20 kilometres south of the city.

Between June 2004 and May 2006, the police discovered the bodies of six more women who had led high-risk lifestyles in the city. The body of Rachel Quinney, 19, was found in a wooded area near Sherwood Park in June 2004. Months later, the frozen remains of Samantha Tayleen Berg, 19, also a sex-trade worker, were found in a parking lot in Edmonton's north side.

Three months after Berg's body was found, the burned remains of Charlene Gauld, 20, were found in a field near Camrose, approximately 80 kilometres southeast of Edmonton. Ellie May Meyer's remains were found near Sherwood Park in April 2005, and the body of Bonnie Lynn Jack, aka Bonny Lynn Loyie, was found in the same general area in May 2006.

The discovery Theresa Innes' remains in a hockey bag at a Fort Saskatchewan residence in 2006 brought

the total number of murdered women since 1983 to
21, all women who had led high-risk lifestyles.

⟡

In 2002 while the RCMP were investigating the
separate deaths of Pitre, Munch, Ballantyne and Lake,
a separate investigation was also going on behind the
scenes.

The Joint Missing Women's Task Force in Vancouver was just beginning to mount its case against Robert William Pickton, accused in the murder of 26
Downtown Eastside prostitutes, when, as Sekela put
it, "we proactively looked in our own backyard."

Project KARE was initially not known by that name.
Instead, it was called the High-Risk Missing Persons
Project, a joint project between the RCMP and differ-
ent municipal policing detachments not only in
Alberta, but also in the Northwest Territories, Nuna-
vut, Manitoba and Saskatchewan.

"We have thousands of reports of missing persons
every day, and most of them return home. In any
missing persons case or homicides where the circumstances were suspicious, we had flags go up. Our job
was to paint a picture and then if required hang it
up—an investigative component."

The painting, when it was finally completely,
revealed that the RCMP had 40 unsolved homicides
and 38 missing persons reports of both men and
women leading high-risk lifestyles. The investigation
was not just limited to sex-trade workers. Anyone

whose lifestyle, behaviour or circumstances placed him or her at a high risk to be a victim of violent crime—whether a prostitute, a gang member or a hitchhiker—as examined under the mandate of the High-Risk Missing Persons Project.

Members of the project began collecting paper and computer files from all 78 cases and inputting all of the data from those files into a modern database that could link key words or common facts or elements from different files. The system, said Sekela, links anything that two or more files might have in common from the words—persons, places, vehicles or businesses. Staffers spent months inputting hundreds of thousands of pages into the system, working from cases that often had a dozen boxes of written case files associated with them. Every day, on an hourly basis, the computer system automatically conducts a search, scouring its files for common links between files.

The analysis of the files revealed that some of the 40 homicides and 38 missing persons cases were likely related. The exact number of related cases, however, has never been made public. With the information gathering and analysis of the High-Risk Missing Persons Project completed, the task force moved into the investigation phase, announcing the formation of Project KARE in October 2003.

Although it started with nine full-time officers in 2003, the project quickly expanded and integrated to 21 investigators. It has since expanded and is further integrated to include more than 50 full-time investigators and support staff, including full-time partners from the Edmonton Police Service. The investigators were acquired from all over western Canada and include some who worked on the Green Ribbon Task Force and Project Evenhanded—the Pickton farm investigation. There have been many secondments of other police investigators from police forces such as the Blood Tribe Police Service, Lethbridge Police Service, Lacombe Police Department and the Camrose Police Service.

The investigation, however, takes a larger, more integrated approach than traditional investigations. Early on in its inception, Project KARE launched what it calls its Insurgence (or Proactive) Team. The idea was originally to use the team to help gather intelligence from the women working the streets in Edmonton. Teams of investigators started patrolling the area in plainclothes, establishing contacts and relationships with the streetwalkers. The idea progressed from simply collecting intelligence to promoting a feeling of trust between the women on the street and the police, a factor that was often lacking in other investigations across the country. The Insurgence Team members check up on the women, offering cash cards for food and lodgings as well as providing contact information for social agencies to try to get sex workers off of the streets for good. Also, members follow up on information provided to the task force by the women concerning the well being and current status of other women working the streets.

Shortly after the Insurgence Team began its work, Project KARE also began asking the women working the streets to provide photos, information on distinguishable marks or tattoos and samples of their DNA. The reason behind the requests is a depressing reminder of the type of work that Project KARE is involved in. The DNA samples are held on file so that if any of the women turn up dead, they can be more quickly identified. The collection plan has already twice yielded results: both Charlene Gauld and Ellie May Meyer had registered with Project KARE, which made identifying their remains easier. To date, approximately 400 street workers have provided a combination of tombstone data and samples to the task force.

"The girls know they are living a high-risk lifestyle," said Sekela. "It is sad. We had some senior investigators say it wouldn't work, but we have 90 percent compliance for registration from the girls so far."

The Insurgence Team has not only helped get some of the women off the street, but it also developed a strong relationship between the prostitutes and the police.

"We now have girls that will phone us and let us know that they will be gone for a month," said Constable Tamara Bellamy, one of Project KARE's investigators.

Project KARE's formation seemed to confirm what the Edmonton media had been suggesting for years— that there was a serial killer at work. In June 2005, the task force admitted there was possibly a serial offender who was responsible for more than one of the killings, but there was likely more than one person responsible for the total number of homicides that fell under their mandate. The task force defined a serial offender as anyone who kills more than once, with a "cooling off" period in between killings. Project KARE also released a profile of the serial offender they believed was at work. The suspect, reported the profile, is male, probably drives a reliable, high-mileage truck, van or sport utility vehicle and is comfortable driving in rural areas. He also might clean his vehicle at odd times of the day. He likes to hunt, fish or camp or participate in other outdoor activities. He likely has a past or present connection to the area south of Edmonton, including Leduc, Camrose and New Sarepta. Project KARE is offering a $100,000 reward for any information leading to the arrest of a suspect.

"These techniques in isolation won't solve the crimes," said Sekela. "It will be the guys and girls on the street doing old-fashioned police work that will solve these crimes."

According to Sekela, the investigators on the task force have interviewed and researched the backgrounds of "hundreds of persons of interest and hundreds have been eliminated at this time." Each person suspected of involvement in the killings of women who led high-risk lifestyles is interviewed by detectives and subsequently scored based on the information. Within the elimination–removal process, suspects are then categorized under one of four possible options: positively eliminated, for example, the person is dead or incarcerated and couldn't be responsible; probably eliminated, for example, the person has a solid alibi subjected to corroboration by homicide investigators, using tools such as a lie-detector test, and is eliminated as a suspect; requires follow up, as the person is likely not responsible based on information collected in the interview; or the person can't be eliminated for one reason or another as a person of interest.

"They might have a horrendous record for assaults and soliciting, for example," said Sekela. "They might have been arrested for a criminal offence related to high-risk lifestyle behaviours, soliciting or we receive tips as benign as a person who might treat their female children strangely. We interview them before we can entertain eliminating them as persons of interest."

Following the discovery of Rachel Quinney's body in a clump of trees in Sherwood Park on June 11, 2004, Project KARE became the lead investigative body whenever a woman who led a high-risk lifestyle is found dead in the capital region.

To date, the only patterns discernible relate to the high-risk lifestyle the victims led and the location in which many of the bodies were found. Since 1983, 13 of the 21 victims were found east and south of Edmonton in areas around Sherwood Park, Fort Saskatchewan and Leduc. Although several of the victims were of First Nations descent, Sekela explained that this fact is more a function of the number of Aboriginal women who end up working in the sex-trade than any real pattern when it comes to victimology.

"If you look at the number of women on the streets, First Nations people make up the higher percentage of women per capita who lead high-risk lifestyles in accordance with our definition," said Sekela. "By virtue of the numbers that are out there, like any high-risk individual there is an increased likelihood that they could become victims."

Project KARE is not limiting its scope just to women who have turned up dead. Investigators have also issued press releases asking for information on three women who have been reported missing under potentially suspicious circumstances.

In January 2005, the task force asked the public for information about Corrie Renee Ottenbreit, 27. The blue-eyed redhead was last seen in May 2004 and was associated with the sex-trade industry in Edmonton. Maggie Lee Burke, 21, of First Nations descent, was reported missing on December 18, 2004, nine days after she was last seen. She was also a known sex-trade worker. In October 2005, the task force issued a press release concerning the current whereabouts of Delores Dawn Brower, a 33-year-old Métis woman nicknamed "Spider." She was last seen hitchhiking in the early morning hours of May 13, 2004, on 118 Avenue near 70 Street in Edmonton. In all three cases, the police believe there might be foul play involved.

The scope of the investigation is broad, but so too is Project KARE's focus. Each person of interest has to be treated with equal attention if investigators hope to find a strong suspect.

"We developed a system based on investigational experience of the detectives, evidence and behavioural science," said Sekela. "We don't throw out common sense. We don't have tunnel vision. We explore all reasonable avenues of investigation to the fullest extent possible regardless of their origin."

When the day comes that Project KARE arrests a suspect for one or more of the murders they are currently investigating, the task force will be prepared. They already have a full-time special prosecutor working with them. Several members of the team are dedicated full time to preparing disclosure for defence attorneys so that when the time comes, the wheels of justice will begin turning as quickly as possible.

To date, Project KARE has made one arrest, that of Thomas George Svelka. It is a small positive step in the overall investigative process for Project KARE, said Sekela, but an important one that will help drive the team to continue its work.

"We now have the framework for a permanent capacity in Alberta to deal with serial offenders, high-risk missing persons and historic homicides. In every case, we're dealing with someone's relative, and many times people assume that, because the victims are sex-trade workers, we don't care. Everyone in this office cares."

Notes on Sources

Boyd, Neil. *The Last Dance: Murder In Canada.* Scarborough: Prentice Hall, 1988.

Cashman, John. *The Gentleman from Chicago.* New York: Harper & Row, 1973.

Davey, Frank. *Karla's Web: A Cultural Investigation of the Mahaffy–French Murders.* Toronto: Viking, 1994.

Ferry, John, and Damian Inwood. *The Olson Murders.* Langley: Cameo Books, 1982.

Goulding, Warren. *Just Another Indian: A Serial Killer and Canada's Indifference.* Calgary: Fifth House, 2001.

Holmes, Leslie, and Bruce L. Northorp. *Where Shadows Linger: The Untold Story of the RCMP's Olson Murders Investigation.* Surrey: Heritage House, 2000.

Kennedy, Leslie, and Robert Silverman. *Deadly Deeds: Murder in Canada.* Scarborough: Nelson Canada, 1993.

MacLean, Rick, et al. *Terror's End: Allan Legere on Trial.* Toronto: McClelland & Stewart, 1992.

McLaren, Angus. *A Prescription for Murder.* Chicago: University of Chicago Press, 1993.

Mulgrew, Ian. *Final Payoff: The True Price of Convicting Clifford Olson.* Toronto: Seal Books, 1990.

Pron, Nick. *Lethal Marriage: The Uncensored Truth Behind the Crimes of Karla Homolka and Paul Bernardo.* Mississauga: Seal Books, 2005.

Williams, Stephen. *Invisible Darkness: The Strange Case of Paul Bernardo and Karla Homolka.* Toronto: Little Brown and Company, 1996.

Williams, Stephen. *Karla: A Pact with the Devil.* Toronto: Cantos, 2003.

Web Sources

Bouchard-Kerr, Jan. *Clifford Olson: The Case of the Missing Lower Mainland Children.* Retrieved November 5, 2005, from http://www.crimelibrary.com/serial_killers/predators/olson/1.html.

Geringer, Joseph. *Dr. Thomas Neill Cream.* Retrieved June 27, 2006, from http://www.crimelibrary.com/serial_killers/history/cream/index_1.html.

King, Gary C. *Keith Hunter Jesperson: The Happy Face Killer*.
    Retrieved July 25, 2006, from http://www.crimelibrary.
    com/serial_killers/predators/jesperson/murder_1.html.
Newton, Michael. *Robert Pickton: The Vancouver Missing Women*.
    Retrieved May 23, 2006, from http://www.crimelibrary.
    com/serial_killers/predators/robert_pickton/1.html.
Project KARE: Unsolved Homicides/High Risk Missing Persons.
    Retrieved June 16, 2006, from http://www.kare.ca.
Edmonton's Murdered Women. Retrieved June 26, 2006, from
    http://www.cbc.ca/background/edmonton_murders.
The Missing Women of Vancouver. Retrieved May 30, 2006, from
    http://www.cbc.ca/news/background/pickton.
Her Majesty the Queen and Allan Joseph Legere. Retrieved March
    3, 2006, from http://law.unb.ca/library/legere.draft.htm.

Peter Boer

Peter Boer is a journalist, author and history buff. In university, he earned a BA in psychology and went on to complete a graduate degree in journalism. He now works as a reporter for the *St. Albert Gazette* in St. Albert, Alberta. He is also the author of *Bush Pilots: Daredevils of the Wilderness* and *Canadian Spies and Spies in Canada: Undercover at Home and Abroad. Canadian Crime Investigations* is his fourth book for Folklore Publishing.